G.O.A.T.

(GOSPEL OF AFRONOMICS THEOLOGY)

G.O.A.T.

(GOSPEL OF AFRONOMICS THEOLOGY)

A 21ST CENTURY BLUEPRINT FOR BLACK ECONOMIC POWER

Brother Minister Zumbi Y. Shawala

G.O.A.T. (Gospel of Afronomics Theology)

Disclaimer: This publication is designed to provide the reader with competent and reliable information on the subject matter. However, it is sold with the understanding that the author and publisher are not engaged in offering legal, financial, or other professional advice. Laws and practices vary from state to state and nation to nation. If expert advice is required, the services of a professional should be sought. The author and publisher expressly disclaim any liability incurred from the use or application of the contents of this book.

For information contact:
Liberty Hall Media Group
240 State St. #2452
Albany, NY 12220
www.libhallmedia.com
E-Mail: **libertyhallpress@gmail.com**

Cover design by Grafiz Designs (**www.fiverr.com/grafiz_designs**)
ISBN: (paperback): 978-1-62676-555-9
First Edition: January 2021

10 9 8 7 6 5 4 3 2

Dedication

I dedicate this book to my ancestral teacher, Brother Steve Cokely (PBUH). I was introduced to your work in 1989 through an interview with Bob Law on WBLS Radio (NYC). You were having a dialogue with Jonathan Kaufman over Black-Jewish relations. Since that interview, I became a follower of your work.

In 1994, I met you live for the first time at Austin Peay State University in Clarksville, TN. You were discussing your thoughts on the Quibilah Shabazz situation. The dialogue was very insightful. That encounter led me to begin doing personal research of the world as it is and how to improve it. In 2002, our paths crossed again at SUNY-Albany. That was the time I became a "student" of yours. There were things you taught us that continue to have a far-reaching impact on my life.

The single greatest jewel you gave us was when you came to SUNY-Albany with Dr. Leonard Jefferies in November 2002. We were at the Best Western Hotel, and you taught us about having character, honor, and integrity when choosing to be a servant of African people. You reminded us to never come before the people dirty. That resonated with me then and now. I pay that lesson forward to a new generation of young African men.

I also took the lessons of creating a "Freedom Fighters University," along with the need for black futurists. As I continue to carry that mission through Liberty Hall Academy, I ask that your spirit continue to guide and assist me and others who sat at your feet and now move forward.

I thank you for your time, insight, humor, lessons, and transparency with your life. May I continue to bring the message live and uncensored. Check!

I also dedicate this book to the independent spirits of Oscar Micheaux (PBUH), Sam Greenlee (PBUH)(**THE SPOOK WHO SAT BY THE DOOR**), Tariq Nasheed (**HIDDEN COLORS** series), Omar Shabazz (Shabazz Productions), Raheim Shabazz (**ELEMENTARY SUICIDE** seris) and Melvin Van Peebles (**SWEET SWEETBACK'S BADDASSS SONG**). By choosing the route of independence to produce your respective works, you have given me the confidence and the blueprint to "do for self" and show our people we can tell our story our way with our money.

My dedication also includes the independent hip-hop group Precise Science of Baltimore. Ruff Mic and Freedom Writer have demonstrated how a culturally conscious rap duo can choose to be independent and deliver their message to the people "live and uncensored."

Table of Contents

Foreword

I have known Chris Johnson (Zumbi Y. Shawala) for many years and watched him research, write and live the contained in this monumental book.

In this age of computer-generated books, it is very rare to find an author who truly puts in the time, effort, and passion to develop a guidebook for the next generation of African-American leaders and thinkers.

Chris has been an eager student of many great thinkers and writers who has helped him develop and codify these unique principles of entrepreneurship and wealth building. He has incorporated the wisdom and principles of classic economists and filtering them through the practical philosophies of black titans of the business world.

In this book, Chris has distilled complex economic principles (wisdom of the ages) into specific action concepts. He has developed, organized, and written these African-centered principles in a concise, straightforward manner that is easy to understand and apply.

The Gospel of Afronomics Theology provides a spiritual, yet practical approach to solving the riddle of survival so that we can thrive and not just survive. It is a "thinker's book" that gives critical guidance as many African Americans strive to overcome the impact of the COVID-19 pandemic.

This gifted author has put legs on the Kwanzaa principles and filtered through the concepts of Robert Kiyosaki's **RICH DAD POOR DAD** to create a unique approach to economics and wealth building in the 21st century and beyond.

The Gospel of Afronomics Theology (G.O.A.T.) is a unique book that will guide African Americans and all people of goodwill to a better understanding of money, economics, and spiritual transformation.

Congratulations on a job well done!

Dr. Herbert (H.J.) Harris, CEO

LifeSkill Institute, Inc.

Author of **THE TWELVE UNIVERSAL LAWS OF SUCCESS, HOW TO MAKE MONEY IN MUSIC** and **SOLVING THE RACE ISSUE IN AMERICA**

www.herbertharris.com

Millionaire Mentorship Show (Podcast)

www.bshaniradio.com/millionaire-mentorship1

Preface

The **GOSPEL OF AFRONOMICS THEOLOGY** provides an economic blueprint for African people for the 21st century and beyond. This book conveys my research, experience, and observation of African people in economics, politics, education, business, and entrepreneurship.

THE GOSPEL OF AFRONOMICS THEOLOGY presents principles that will help African people to become financially independent at an individual and collective level. It consists of 60 basic principles and a Q & A with myself about the G.O.A.T. philosophy.

The book was inspired by a need to create an economic blueprint for African people. Since 1865,

African people in America have amassed a gross domestic product of approximately $1.7 trillion. Yet, 44% of America's homeless are African men. We have no medical centers, think tanks, or industries we own and control. Also, 98% of African people in America work for non-African entities, be it the corporate, nonprofit, or government sectors. How can this be with the kind of wealth we have amassed?

In my research and personal experience, everyone has addressed and analyzed the problem to no end. In fact, I dare say that some have built careers off identifying the problem and have not offered a practical solution, program, or system to address the economic issues afflicting our people.

I have also researched some of the solutions proposed by others who study economics and business. Their programs were either obsolete, too theoretical, or required a significant mass of people to move. **THE GOSPEL OF AFRONOMICS**

THEOLOGY became a list of principles for African people to follow and embrace. The list was initially seven principles in 2006. Since then, the list has grown to 60 principles, 16 Core Beliefs, Ten Commandments of G.O.A.T., and a C.H.I.C.A.G.O. Code. The X-factor in building wealth became the culture. If you show me a set of people who have cultural cohesiveness, I'll show you a set of economically prosperous people. Culture, history, and spirituality are the nucleus in developing a people's economic prosperity.

This book series will also explain the roles of politics, education, and psychology play in a people's quest for economic prosperity.

If one were to ask me how I would describe the **GOSPEL OF AFRONOMICS THEOLOGY**, I would say it is a guide for African people to embrace a new economic reality. I would define **AFRONOMICS** as the science of the study and application of economic principles influenced by an African-centered paradigm. I want African people to envision a reality of being producers instead of consumers. I want African people to envision owning and controlling the means of their production and enjoying the fruits of their labor. For too long, African people have served as the raw material that fueled the construction of other people's empires and kingdoms. Now, we must learn to use our tangible and intangible resources to enrich ourselves.

The Honorable Elijah Muhammad predicted there would come a day when white people cannot employ themselves, and we can bear witness to that reality now. Globalization, downsizing, outsourcing, automation, robotics, and privatization have forever shifted the global economy. What does this mean for African people? Can African people continue to think along the lines of begging for entry into someone else's empire for provision? Or, do African people begin to apply their tangible and intangible resources towards their economic liberation?

The best way to use **THE GOSPEL OF AFRONOMICS THEOLOGY** is to read the entire book series. Then, read it again and begin to form your own personal economic blueprint and wealth-building formula. Each volume addresses a different aspect of wealth building from an African-centered perspective. I recommend you take notes while reading each volume because you will greatly benefit from active reading. This book series is divided into fourteen volumes:

- ***G.O.A.T. Tablet 1:*** *Core Beliefs*
- ***G.O.A.T. tablet 2****: Ten Commandments of G.O.A.T.*
- ***G.O.A.T. Tablet 3****: The C.H.I.C.A.G.O. Code*
- ***G.O.A.T. Tablet 4****: Pyramid of Prosperity*
- ***G.O.A.T. Tablet 5****: Wealth Building Quadrant*

- ***G.O.A.T. Tablet 6****: Principles #1-10*
- ***G.O.A.T. Tablet 7****: Principles #11-20*
- ***G.O.A.T. Tablet 8****: Principles #21-30*
- ***G.O.A.T. Tablet 9****: Principles #31-40*
- ***G.O.A.T. Tablet 10****: Principles #41-50*
- ***G.O.A.T. Tablet 11****: Principles #51-60*
- ***G.O.A.T. Tablet 12****: Advisors to the King (or Queen)*
- ***G.O.A.T. Tablet 13****: Get Your Biz Legit*
- ***G.O.A.T. Tablet 14****: S.C.R.I.B.E. of the G.O.A.T.*
- ***G.O.A.T. Tablet 15****: Ten-Point Tax Refundefund Plan*
- ***G.O.A.T. Tablet 16****: Republic of New Palmares*

Each volume will also include a **CALL TO ACTION**. I feel it is necessary to give the reader "homework assignments." After reading a book series of this nature, the reader will ask what s/he can do. I do not want this to be a "feel good" book series that gets parked on the shelf after being read. I want this to serve as an active playbook. There will be suggestions for the reader to consider in taking action. The reader must feel empowered to change his condition and have the opportunity to apply what he has learned to experience victory.

Many times, a reader will read the book and later go to Amazon or some other website to give their review of the book, claiming how bogus the book is. The reality is that they never applied the book to real-world situations to discover the validity of the book.

I encourage you to put the book to the test. Taking action is the only way to discover what the possibilities are. Taking action allows me to see what is applicable and what needs to be adjusted. I have confidence in **THE GOSPEL OF AFRONOMICS THEOLOGY** and its capacity for change. Read it. Digest it. Put the principles into action, and I promise your economic condition will change for the better.

Enjoy your learning experience.

Brother Minister Zumbi Y. Shawala, S.O.A.P.
(Servant of African People)

Transform Our Communities

1. Stop spending lavishly
2. Learn politics and Ideal Policies **BECAUSE THEY AFFECT YOU**
3. Consume what you control
4. Know that debt is used to control you
5. Put in the **WORK** if you want economic liberation

Thomas Sankara

Acknowledgments

Developing my first book has given me a deeper appreciation of the book writing and self-publishing process. Taking a vision for a book from mind to market is unlike any journey I've experienced. The years of research and personal experience, along with hours of revising this book could not be possible without those who supported me financially, emotionally, and through rigorous dialogue and exchange of ideas.

First, I would like to thank the Universe and the Ancestors for inspiring me to bring this book to life. All ideas have a spark, and I was blessed with this spark. A special acknowledgment must also go to the African World Community. They served not only as the subjects for this book but also the teachers. The people have a way of teaching you what their needs are, how they want those needs to be met, and how those needs are addressed. Hopefully, this book has met the economic requirements of the people in some capacity.

I would like to thank those unborn Africans who are waiting for this book to use as their blueprint for wealth and prosperity. Every time I would write a page, I think of some young African man or woman in the future reading this book and applying the principles to his or her business and financial lives. To know that some Africans will benefit from my work is a profoundly humbling gesture. For those unborn Africans, I thank you and honor you with this book.

I would like to thank my "African disciple" of the G.O.A.T. philosophy, Shaqir "Bilal" Erasmus, who will bring the "Good News" of this economic gospel to the African continent. Although your economic ministry is presently in the Bronx, you will evolve beyond the borders of the five boroughs. You have embraced this philosophy and chose to passionately "spread the gospel" of this black economic liberation theology throughout the African World Community. Thank you…☺☺☺

Many thanks to Corey V. Sapp, Devardo Richards, and Kacy Saile for the weekly men's group. I made promises to those who gave to me that I would "pay it forward". Plus, I also made a promise to never be a "generational thief" and rob your generation of the knowledge and wisdom necessary to grow and evolve.

Many thanks to Robert (Bob) Blackford, June Scalzo, and Lisbeth Calendrino, who I consider three of my better business teachers who gave me great lessons in business. Mr. Blackford taught me so much during my fifteen-month "internship" in his business "incubator". Ms. Scalzo taught me the importance of customer service and never compromising on giving quality customer service. Ms. Calendrino always taught me to create a customer before creating a product. For these lessons, I give you thanks ☺

Special thanks to Grafiz Designs (**www.fiverr.com/grafiz_designs**) for the book cover design. I highly recommend this group for anyone needing quality book formatting and a quality book cover design at a reasonable price. I'll make sure to let everyone know where to go. Thank you for your role in bringing this vision into reality. Like General Electric, Grafiz Designs brings good things to life☺

I also would like to thank BooksMango (**www.fiverr.com/booksmango**) for providing the ISBN and barcode for the paperback and ebook editions of the book. I've always wanted to self-publish a book that looked like a traditionally published book. I feel the customer (and his money) deserves that respect from my books.

Special thanks to Moxesmaxie (**www.fiverr.com/moxesmaxie**) for editing, proofreading, formatting, and publishing the manuscript, and shaping it into a finished and polished product. Finding a quality editor was the most challenging aspect of the self-publishing process. Once I found Moxesmaxie and saw his work, I knew I had my editor. Thank You for taking my raw manuscript and transforming it into a polished product.

Special thanks to Brother Khalifah Muhammad (Nat Turner Library, VA) and Brother Michael and Sister Tangela Muhammad (Nat Turner Radio Show) (**www.bromichaelmuhammad.com**). As contemporaries, we find ourselves coming from different schools of thought to converge on working for the liberation of our people. The Economic Blueprint of the Most Honorable Elijah Muhammad had a significant impact on this economic philosophy. I just want to do justice like the ancestor in the continuance of teaching the science of business, economics, and finance.

Special thanks to Keidi Obi Awadu of LIBRadio/Black Star Media (**www.libradio.com**) and Imam Sheikh Akbar Bilal of New Black Panther Party Black Power Radio (**www.blogtalkradio/freedomordeath**) for opening their platforms to me. I am always grateful to those who allow me the opportunity to bring this message of economic empowerment to the people.

I remember the words of Dr. John Henrik Clarke, who taught that education has one honorable objective: to be a responsible handler of power. In each interview I conduct, I want to be a responsible handler of the power of the media. Thank you ☺

Special thanks to Alberto Delossantos. Through the years, I've learned much from you about leadership through volunteering. Since 2008-09, I've been able to develop leadership skills that transfer well into the business world. Thanks, Al☺

Special thanks to Brother Dell Gines (**www.yourblackeconomy.com**) for his input in shaping and developing this book. He is also someone I highly recommend and endorse for his commitment to black economic development and empowerment. I want to call him "Dr. Gines", as he is working towards his doctorate. Hopefully, as of this writing, he has achieved his goal. He is one of our best and brightest minds in regards to economic development and economic empowerment. His scientific approach to economic development is a real breath of fresh air.

Special thanks to Sister Nataki Gilmore-Cokely, Steve Cokely II (Ajamu Bakari)(**www.themoringamatrix.com**), and the rest of the Cokely family for allowing Brother Steve Cokely (PBUH)to serve us. People forget that every activist and revolutionary must have a support system and family in his corner to fulfill his mission, vision, and purpose. Because of your support, those of us who are students of Brother Cokely can continue the work and run with the ball. Asante Sana for your support.

Shout outs to Maxie D. Collier, who produced the hip-hop entrepreneurship documentary **PAPER CHASERS**, and Kenyatta Griggs, founder of **HIP-**

HOP MOTIVATION (**www.myhiphopmotivation.com**), co-executive producer of **THE SECRET TO BALLIN'** and co-author of **CULTURE VULTURES** (with Damon Dash). You are the manifestation of the ninth element of hip-hip: street entrepreneurship. Through researching a workshop, your content helped me to create a youth-based hip-hop entrepreneurship curriculum. You also played a critical role in the development of Liberty Hall Media Group.

A special thanks goes to Dr. Herbert Harris (**www.herbertharris.com**) for taking the time to contribute the foreword to this book. When an elder you admire and respect gives his endorsement to the work you've done, it is the most humbling feeling that stimulates an outpouring of gratitude. I am always reminded to "pay it forward". As you have paid it forward to me, I will pay it forward to others when the opportunity arises.

May this book serve as a spark to those Africans seeking answers to their economic challenges. I write this book as a humble servant of African people (S.O.A.P.). I present this book before African people as my "gift" for the economic empowerment, upliftment, and liberation of African people. Thank You for your purchase of this book. To be rewarded with compensation for one's life's work is a deeply humbling experience. Your support is a validation of its value to African people

Introduction

Dear Reader:

May this message and book be received in the best of holistic health and spirits.

Welcome to G.O.A.T., or the Gospel of Afronomics Theology. G.O.A.T. is an economic philosophy and system for African people in the 21st century and beyond. To give you an example as to the importance of this book series, here are some numbers to consider.

There is a global economy of over $300 trillion. Every 24 hours, over $1.4 trillion circulates throughout the world seeking a home. The USA has a GDP (gross domestic product) of $19.75 trillion. In America,

African people have a purchasing power of approximately $2 trillion. Yet, 98% of all African people in America work for non-African entities. Only 2% are considered financially independent of a job or some form of government assistance. That is 2 out of every 100, or 1 out of every 50. So, how do you expect to build a new Black Wall Street when the bulk of your time and energy is invested in developing the empires of other people?

I intend to address issues like these and offer a philosophy and system of how to overcome the economic challenges that face African people.

The genesis of G.O.A.T. began in 2006. I was in my living room watching a Deepak Chopra DVD. During the movie, I heard a whispering voice say "AFRONOMICS!" I was the only one at home! From that moment, I began to write economic principles of what African people want and need. Over twelve years, the G.O.A.T. philosophy has evolved into 60 principles, 16 Core Beliefs of G.O.A.T., Ten Commandments of G.O.A.T., in this book. This book is intended to be a book of empowerment, instruction, and inspiration to the reader. After reading this book, the reader should have a "how" and a "why" to make changes in his economic life.

Throughout the book series, the reader will be introduced to the 60 principles of G.O.A.T., the 16 Core Beliefs of G.O.A.T., the Wealth Building Quadrant, the Pyramid of Prosperity and discuss the roles of culture, politics, education, history, spirituality, and "Afrofuturology" in a people's quest for financial freedom and economic independence.

My promise to the reader is to challenge the thought process and force him to think beyond the burdens of his day. Part of how I keep that promise is by challenging the "Sacred Cow" rules of money. Since 1971, America has operated in a fiat economy after Richard Nixon took the US dollar off the gold standard. Also, since 1974, companies would no longer be responsible for an employee's retirement.

My background has been that of a researcher, consultant, coach, thought leader, and entrepreneur. I have also co-hosted and produced my internet radio show for five years, addressing topics in economics, business, entrepreneurship, and self-help. My entrepreneurial experience comes from being a partner in a small independent publishing company. That experience gave me the confidence to launch Liberty Hall Media Group. Now, I am inspired and driven to "give birth" to the G.O.A.T. philosophy.

I intend to provide future generations of African people with a brighter path and a better blueprint for financial freedom and economic independence. I have seen what has not been done concerning collectively improving the economic condition of African people. I have been told that this is one of the more pragmatic "blueprints" for African people.

Recently, I read **ABOVE THE LINE** by Urban Meyer, former head football coach of the Ohio State University and head coach of the NFL's Jacksonville Jaguars. In the book, Meyer states there are three types of leaders and what they offer to those under their command:

1. Average leaders bring clichés and slogans
2. Good leaders bring a program
3. Exceptional leaders bring a system

I would like to think I am building and proposing a system that will be timeless. I want the G.O.A.T. philosophy to continue influencing African people for the next 100-200 years. My intention is for African people to become serious about the business, financial, and leadership roles in their lives. My plan is for this book series to inform, instruct, inspire and empower African people.

May this book serve as a catalyst for African people to be "forever free" and live life on their own terms.

Brother Minister Zumbi Y. Shawala

From The Honorable Elijah Muhammad's
MESSAGE TO THE BLACKMAN IN AMERICA

"We must begin at the cradle and teach our babies that they must do something for themselves. They must not be like we, their fathers, who look to the slave-masters and the slave master's children for all. We must teach our children now with enthusiasm exceeding that which our slave-masters used in having our forefathers embed the seed of dependency within us. We must stop the process of giving our brainpower, labor, and wealth to our slave-masters' children. We must eliminate the master-slave relationship." (Pg. 56-57)

"As I have repeated until my throat is dry, one day America (the white man) will not be able to carry this entire nation of 22 million Black people on her back. Their world is getting very small and if you are dependent upon their world, yours too is getting very small. Self-preservation is the first law of nature. Everyone tries to provide a future of his own but the American so-called Negro." (Pg. 200-01)

"Let's get together, get some land
Raise our food like "the Man"
Save our money like the Mob
Put up a factory And own a job"
James Brown
"**Funky President**" (1974)

The Need For A Black Economic Liberation Theology (B.E.L.T.)

THE NEED FOR A BLACK ECONOMIC LIBERATION THEOLOGY (B.E.L.T.)

The Power of an Idea

The only way a man can be pregnant is if he is "pregnant" with an idea that can change the world. The Honorable Marcus Garvey had an idea of restoring African people to a place of honor and respect amongst the human family. The Honorable Elijah Muhammad had an idea of reminding African people of the divinity within themselves and awakening African people to the divinity within themselves. He said, "Every time I see a black man, I'm looking at God". Each man took his respective idea and created an ideology, philosophy, and theology. They developed a blueprint for how African people can move in the world as a collective force. Both included culture, history, and spirituality to serve as the nucleus of their respective movements.

In regards to economic empowerment, both believed in building industries and institutions to employ African people. Both believed in frugality and pooling resources. Both believed in eliminating vices that could potentially harm one's personal economy (alcohol, tobacco, gambling, etc.). They also believed in the importance of owning and controlling land. By having land, both understood it was and is the basis for all political and economic power.

Both men created a set of core values and core beliefs to serve as a guide to how African people should handle their business and financial lives. Because of their ideas, they were able to demonstrate the possibilities of having industries owned and controlled by the people. They demonstrated what can be done with the confidence in self to go and do for self. They demonstrated what it means to produce goods and services to offer the marketplace and create value. They demonstrated how to create our own bakeries and producing our own baked goods instead of begging for crumbs, scraps, and leftovers from another man's table.

With these examples, African people have a proven blueprint for economic empowerment. We can study, apply and adjust the blueprint to fit our time. Marcus Garvey commanded us to rise and accomplish what we will. Let us fulfill that assignment.

Core Beliefs and Commandments

In developing a Black Economic Liberation Theology, one must have a set of core beliefs that serve as the foundation. The Gospel of Afronomics Theology has a set of core beliefs that establishes an economic belief system that African people can embrace, internalize and manifest:

1. We believe the Universe built man to be self-employed and entrepreneurial.
2. We believe one must know oneself to master oneself, one's life, one's emotions, and one's resources.
3. We believe poverty is "Hell on Earth".
4. We believe money is neither good nor evil, but simply a tool.
5. We believe welfare is an insidious form of slavery.
6. We believe in education, but an education that teaches African people to be producers instead of consumers.
7. We believe there must be an entrepreneurial revolution amongst African people, especially men.
8. We believe a people's true wealth is not in land, but its collective consciousness.

9. We believe culture, history, and spirituality are the nucleus of a people's economic prosperity.
10. We believe in creating generational wealth for our posterity.
11. We believe in the economic self-reliance and self-sufficiency of African people.
12. We believe in the individual and collective financial prosperity of African people.
13. We believe wealth is the result of man's ability to organize and maximize his resources.
14. We believe wealth creation must always be pursued from a place of "moral superiority".
15. We believe wealth creation must involve creating and increasing value in the marketplace.
16. We believe African people must create wealth to share it.

This set of core beliefs answers the question of what African people believe is for their economic highest and greatest good. It gives African people a set of ideas for which to strive. It also forces African people to undergo a process of becoming a people in alignment with these core beliefs.

The Gospel of Afronomics Theology also includes its "Ten Commandments". These commandments are:

1. Thou shalt decide and commit to becoming rich and wealthy.
2. Thou shalt invest in learning and mastering the Science of Money
3. Thou shalt practice the 10% Solution
4. Thou shalt create value in the market
5. Thou shalt build wealth with passive and residual income.
6. Thou shalt respect the power of money.
7. Thou shalt treat money as thy servant.
8. Thou shalt have a wealth-building plan and wealth protection plan.

9. Thou shalt practice "cultural tithing".
10. Thou shalt master thyself and thy emotions.

A good theology is one that encourages an individual to strive to operate from his or her Higher Self. A good theology also impresses upon the individual the need to change his behavior. The change must take place at a deep level to experience a transformation or "reality reconstruction". Real change is experienced first at the ether level. The next experience comes at the psychic level and, finally, the material level.

The G.O.A.T. Flag

Every theology has symbols to represent itself. The G.O.A.T. philosophy is acknowledged by having a flag as one of its symbols. The G.O.A.T. flag is comprised of four colors: 1) Red, 2) Black, 3) Gold and 4) Green. Red symbolizes the blood of African people.

It represents the bloodshed for the upliftment of African people. It also represents the blood that carries the ancestral memories throughout our DNA. Black represents the people of the African Diaspora. Peter Tosh said no matter where we are if we are black, we are African.

We have discovered our presence not only in Africa but in Asia, Europe, the South Pacific, and ancient America (North and South). We are over one billion strong throughout the earth. We are not "minorities" because there is nothing minor about us as a people or our experiences in human history. Our ancient greatness is well documented, as are our accomplishments and achievements today.

Regardless of our present condition, we have never been a "poor" people. Not only do we possess financial wealth, but also cultural and spiritual wealth. Our labor has served as the backbone of the Industrial

Revolution, Wall Street, and the American Sports Empire.

As we awaken to our authentic selves, we will begin to harness our wealth and enrich ourselves and, ultimately, humanity. Green is for the land. We have been blessed with a continent rich in fertile soil for crops and minerals for manufacturing and technology. Dr. Khalid Abdul Muhammad (PBUH) said the earth is our home and Africa is our throne.

The Honorable Elijah Muhammad teaches that land is the basis of **ALL** political and economic power. He encouraged us to get some of this "good earth" to call our own. The land gives us trees to make products from wood. It gives us our food supply, cotton for clothing, and minerals for manufacturing.

Purpose

Why is a B.E.L.T. (Black Economic Liberation Theology) necessary? My feeling is that African people need an economic philosophy that speaks to the economic challenges and issues facing us. In the Oxford American Dictionary (2nd Edition), theology is defined as a "system of religious beliefs and theory". One can look at G.O.A.T. and see it as a theology for economic empowerment and liberation. Having a B.E.L.T. creates a system of beliefs and theories about black economic empowerment. It organizes thoughts and beliefs about money systematically.

The benefits of having a B.E.L.T. include having a guide to organizing thoughts about money and economics, looking at B.E.L.T. and G.O.A.T. through an African-centered paradigm, understanding how economics should work for us, and reinforcing the importance of production overconsumption.

A good economic theology encourages people to strive for a better life and a better future. Having a set of economic principles that cut through all schools of thought helps solve the riddle of unity without uniformity.

Need

There are three needs for a black economic liberation theology (B.E.L.T.) :1) Need for a framework, 2) Need for a clearly defined endgame, and 3) Need for a practice and a process. The need for a framework is to create structure and organize core beliefs, core values, and knowledge and information. The need for an endgame is to get over 60 million African people in America on the same page via a plebiscite or other means to have a consensus on what the economic endgame should be. Do we want reparations? Liberation? Or, 40 acres, two mules, and $100 cash? What **EXACTLY** do African people want economically? Until we are clear on the endgame, we will continue to operate from fear, greed, ignorance, and confusion.

Finally, the need for a practice and a process is critical. What good is it for any of us to have resources and lack the knowledge of the practice and process to convert those resources into wealth? For every cause, there is an effect. Money is the effect, and the practice and process are the cause. The practice and process are where **REAL** change occurs. The practice and process will last longer than the prize. For the Israelites to become a free people and take control of the Promised Land, they had to endure the practice and process of thinking, speaking, and acting as a free people. They also had to detoxify themselves of the colonized mindset and slave spirit that was imposed on them during their captivity. Part of that detoxification included older generations to pass away for younger generations who are more in alignment with a freedom mentality.

Benefits

The benefits of having a clearly defined black economic liberation theology are direction, instruction, and flexibility. Having a clear sense of direction allows the individual to focus on his business and financial goals, or "targets". All ambiguity and vagueness are removed when the direction and "endgame" is clear. The instruction is the "how-to" aspect of B.E.L.T.

Instruction shortens the learning curve and minimizes the need for trial-and-error experimentation. Instruction gives the individual guidance on his journey to financial independence. Instruction helps keep the individual on the "straight and narrow" and keeps deviation to a minimum. Flexibility is a key component in the journey of economic liberation. One must be flexible in the tactics and strategies used. One may begin with a certain formula, only to realize it is no longer effective. That is where flexibility is necessary. The goal or objective remains the same, but the formula changes. As Clint Eastwood said in **HEARTBREAK RIDGE**: "Adapt, adjust, overcome!"

Core Beliefs

TABLET #1:

Core Beliefs

"It's the repetition of affirmations that leads to belief. And once that belief becomes a deep conviction, things begin to happen."

- *Muhammad Ali*

Every philosophy must have a set of core beliefs to establish itself. The Core Beliefs of G.O.A.T intend to establish ideals for those who choose to embrace and practice this philosophy. No one has to leave his church, synagogue, masjid, temple, or tabernacle. No one has to change political parties. This black economic liberation theology is compatible with any religious philosophy that advocates self-empowerment, self-reliance, and self-sufficiency. This also eliminates the need for division and conflict because economics impacts every aspect of human life.

1. **We believe the Universe built man to be self-employed and entrepreneurial**: Entrepreneurship and microenterprise are the

keys to bringing African people from poverty to prosperity. The Honorable Elijah Muhammad predicted there will come a day when white people cannot employ their own. The time is now for African people to produce jobs for themselves and stop begging other races for employment and provision. Baba Omowale (Malcolm X) said when you depend upon your enemy for a job, you're in bad shape. Our "liberation fitness" needs an overhaul.

2. **We believe one must know oneself in order to master oneself, one's emotions, and one's resources**: Warren Buffett states if you cannot control your emotions, you cannot control your money. Money is an emotional topic that triggers a wide range of emotions. As you begin to know, understand and master yourself and your life, you will begin to master your money

3. **We believe poverty is "Hell on Earth"**: The Honorable Marcus Garvey states that poverty is a hellish condition. There is **NOTHING** honorable in Poverty. Aristotle said poverty is the parent of revolution and crime. Being poor and impoverished opens the door to crime, hell, and death. Poverty is a despicable state of being.

4. **We believe money is neither good nor evil, but a tool**: Money is a neutral tool. How it is used depends on the person who possesses it and the consciousness behind it. Money has been used for the construction of schools, hospitals, and libraries. So money can do good things. Stop player hating on money!

5. **We believe welfare is an insidious form of slavery**: Ideally, the welfare system is to serve as a "bridge" for people who have fallen on hard

times and need a "hand up" to get back on their feet. What has happened is that welfare has become an insidious form of slavery and an industry. The system rewards laziness and punishes initiative and drive. In many ways, welfare has become an industry that is only concerned with justifying its own existence. Liberation threatens that industry.

6. **We believe in education, but an education that teaches us to be producers**: Education should not be a journey to employment, but empowerment. To go and do something for self. The proper education should empower the student. Instead, the present school system trains the students to be employees and soldiers, operating from the seed of dependency planted in them. Real education leads to liberation.

7. **We believe there must be an entrepreneurial revolution amongst African people, especially men**: If African people are serious about becoming the #1 employer of African people, then an entrepreneurial revolution is a must so we can begin to employ our people en masse. Also, with a disproportionate number of African males either unemployed or underemployed, the pursuit of entrepreneurship must become the first priority instead of a desperate last resort.

8. **We believe a people's true wealth is not in the land, but in its collective consciousness**: Land is like knowledge. It is **NOT** power, but **POTENTIAL** power. What makes land valuable is knowing what is in the land, how to extract the minerals and raw materials from the land, and how to cultivate fertile land and plant and grow crops for food. African people must not only

acquire land but also learn how to make land an asset for themselves. The Honorable Elijah Muhammad instructed us to get some of this good earth to call our own. Let us follow the instruction of wise counsel and claim some fertile land that we own and control.

9. **We believe culture, history, and spirituality are the nucleus of a people's economic prosperity**: Show me a people who have cultural, historical, and spiritual cohesiveness and I will show you an economically prosperous people. The Japanese and European Jews are prime examples of cohesiveness. Both groups suffered atrocities. Yet, both groups were able to maintain their nucleus and are now economic forces in the global market. African people must have a strong nucleus in order to experience economic prosperity.

10. **We believe in creating generational wealth for our posterity**: African people can no longer afford to make each generation start from zero every 20-30 years. There can be no long-term wealth built over time if African people do not bequeath the tangible and intangible resources to the next generation. It is the responsibility of the present generation to prepare the future with resources to build the next reality.

11. **We believe in the economic self-reliance and self-sufficiency of African people**: African people must pay "freedom dues" as the Israelites did when they left Egypt. In order to stand as an independent people, African people must foster interdependence within the race. African people cannot rely on the "hookup" or handout. They must think, speak and act like other independent people. Equality comes when you can do for

yourself what other races are doing for themselves.

12. **We believe in the individual and collective financial prosperity of African people**: Many speak of the need for African people to practice group economics. However, the self-economics cannot be ignored or denied. One cannot contribute what he does not have. Group and self-economics go hand in hand. A healthy vibrant personal economy is the cornerstone of a healthy, vibrant group economy.

13. **We believe wealth is the result of man's ability to organize and maximize his resources**: While the wealth creator and builder is acquiring his resources, he must also develop and execute a plan of organizing and maximizing those resources to achieve financial freedom and

economic independence. In many cases, the amount of resources is secondary to how they are organized and positioned to achieve certain financial objectives.

14. **We believe wealth creation must always be pursued from a place of "moral superiority"**: The wealth creator and builder must conduct himself with "moral superiority" in his dealings with the people. "Moral superiority" means that the wealth builder is on his "best behavior' in his personal and business dealings, operating from a place of the utmost character, honor, humility, and integrity in all his business and personal financial dealings. Building an impeccable reputation in business can prove to be your greatest asset. That reputation can open doors and create opportunities for you.

15. **We believe wealth creation must involve creating and increasing value in the marketplace**: Wealth creation and building must include the ability to create and/or increase value in the marketplace. In other words, solving problems for large groups of people. Henry Ford solved the problem of the common man to afford and own a car like the rich. Steve Jobs solved the problem of placing a desktop computer in every home. See what problems need to be solved in the marketplace.

16. **We believe African people must create wealth in order to share it**: People talk about how wealth should be shared. The problem is that someone must create wealth in order to share it. One cannot share what he does not have. The poor cannot help the poor because they do not

have the resources to do so. Fill your tank first in order to fill others.

TABLET #2: Ten commandments of G.O.A.T.

"The Ten Commandments were not a suggestion."

- *Pat Riley*

Everyone has heard of the Ten Commandments. These were the tablets that Moses received from God after staying forty days and forty nights on Mount Sinai. These laws were to govern the Israelites as they emerged from bondage in Egypt. These laws also gave the Israelites a moral compass as to how to treat each other and how to worship God.

In the Gospel of Afronomics Theology, there are "ten commandments" that govern the wealth builder's business and personal financial life. These are laws for African people to incorporate and practice daily. It is one thing to think and say "I am prosperous". It is another to have a prosperity plan and execute that plan.

The Ten Commandments of G.O.A.T. are:

1. **Thou shalt decide and commit to becoming rich and wealthy**: All change begins with a decision. We are inspired to change or are desperate for change. In either case, change begins with deciding to become rich and wealthy.

2. **Thou shalt invest in learning and mastering the science of money**: Proverbs 17:16 asks "What good is it for a man to get paper if he lacks the desire to learn how to master his paper?" Money does not make you rich. It is the mindset, language, and behavior of the individual that determines whether he becomes rich or poor.

3. **Thou shalt practice the 10% Solution**: W. Clement Stone said one must master this habit to discover the seeds of greatness within him.

Paying yourself first is one of the basic habits to develop on the wealth-building journey. It creates a surplus budget.

4. **Thou shalt create value in the market**: Wealth comes through creating value in the marketplace. Find a problem in the market and fill it. Either fill a demand or create one.

5. **Thou shalt build wealth with passive and residual income**: Warren Buffet said one must solve the riddle of how to make money in one's sleep. If you don't, you will work for money all the days of your life. Wealth does not come from a paycheck.

6. **Thou shalt respect the power of money**: Treat money with the respect one would respect a gun, knife, or fire. Money is a tool that can build or

destroy. Money creates choices and amplifies who you are at your core. When you receive money, show gratitude and strive to be a good steward of it.

7. **Thou shalt treat money as thy servant**: Bishop TD Jakes says money is not the mission but funds the mission. Money is to serve you. You were never meant to serve money. Money is like a habit: if you are firm with it and give it direction, it will be a most effective servant. If you are lackadaisical or loose in your treatment of it, money can be a brutal taskmaster and ultimately destroy you for your ignorance of how money works.

8. **Thou shalt have a wealth-building plan and a wealth protection plan**: Financial freedom, economic independence, and financial security

are necessary to ensure generational wealth. Financial freedom and economic independence give you the mindset and resources to make choices and acquire income-generating assets. Financial security gives you peace of mind that your assets are protected from financial predators (legal and illegal). Both are necessary to ensure multigenerational wealth.

9. **Thou shalt practice "cultural tithing"**: African people must give a "cultural tithe" to a "race first" organization whose mission is the upliftment and improvement of African people. Be it religious, cultural, educational, or other entity, African people need to give 10% of every dollar to these organizations that serve the people.

10. **Thou shalt master thyself and thy emotions**: Warren Buffet states if you cannot control your emotions, you cannot control your money. Money is an emotional subject, and emotions are 25 times more powerful than logic. When you lack emotional and fiscal maturity, your money will divorce you without hesitation. Mastery of self and emotions allows the wealth builder to make "intelligent boss moves", says our brother Damon Dash.

These commandments are to serve as guidelines and principles for African people to apply and practice in their business and personal financial lives. Throughout our sojourn towards economic liberation, there have been those who pretended to come in the spirit of MAAT and brotherhood/sisterhood, only to be nothing more than Hotep Hustlers, Black Power Pimps, and Pimpostor Preachers. These predators have brought nothing but destruction and devastation to African people by using culture to rob and rape the people of its financial resources.

If African people are serious about their economic liberation, then they must begin to deal with each other morally and ethically. African people cannot rob one another and expect prosperity to be the result of such mistreatment. They may approach the people as producers, providers, and protectors of the village, but in reality, have become predators and bloodsuckers. They create no value for the people. They do not advance the economic well-being of the people.

TABLET #3:

The C.H.I.C.A.G.O. Code

"A man without ethics is a wild beast loosed upon this world."

Albert Camus

Every aspiring wealth builder needs a bushido, or code of conduct. The Gospel of Afronomics Theology is no different. A bushido is the essential ingredient. These virtues of the C.H.I.C.A.G.O. Code govern every aspect of his business and personal financial life.

I would tell young women not to engage in an intimate relationship with a man who lacks laws that govern his conduct or behavior. The same goes for the aspiring wealth builder. If you have no code of conduct to guide your moral behavior towards money, you create a Michael Milkin. You produce a Bernie Madoff. You have Hotep Hustlers, Black Power Pimps, and Pimpostor Preachers running rampant among us.

But a new era is here. It will be an era where the people would be tired of being exploited. The people will demand greater responsibility and accountability from those who claim to serve them. And the punishment for "intentional misappropriation of funds" will be so severe until the culprit will be treated the same as one who commits treason and will be regarded as an "enemy of the State".

The Eight Virtues of the C.H.I.C.A.G.O. Code are:

1. **Character**: The aspiring wealth builder must display excellent character in his financial dealings with the people he has committed to serve and defend. An aspiring wealth builder must be willing to have the moral excellence and firmness to defend the economic integrity and welfare of African people against all enemies, foreign and domestic.

2. **Honor**: The aspiring wealth builder must develop a reputation of honesty and fair dealing in his financial affairs. The wealth builder is to be held in high esteem by the people because of his/her conduct. He must also make his word his bond in all financial dealings.

3. **Integrity**: The aspiring wealth builder must operate with moral soundness and adherence to the C.H.I.C.A.G.O. Code. The wealth builder must operate from a place of financial wholeness in thought, word, and deed. The wealth builder must come from a place of credibility and congruency in dealing with the people.

4. **Courage**: The aspiring wealth builder must master his fear of the unknown in the pursuit of financial independence. Perseverance, persistence, and the discipline to apply new

habits to one's business and financial life are critical factors in the success of transforming how to think about money.

5. **Action-Oriented**: The aspiring wealth builder takes massive action towards financial freedom. He understands that financial freedom requires work. The wealth builder is not about "showbiz liberation", but about doing the work that is away from the camera, microphone and stage.

6. **Goal-Oriented**: The aspiring wealth builder is about getting his/her business and financial goals accomplished and teaching others to the same. The path to financial freedom must clearly define his goals with a deadline. He must always have a "target" to hit. Focus and discipline are the keys to achieving and accomplishing financial freedom.

7. **Organization:** The aspiring wealth builder must strive to organize his/her financial life and be an example of leading a financially organized life. He must demonstrate habits that bring order to his financial life and show others how to organize their financial lives.

8. **Ethical Excellence**: The aspiring wealth builder is to practice ethical excellence among the people s/he intends to serve and defend economically. He must practice compassion, kindness, and ethical conduct regarding the financial health of African people. He must demonstrate and teach African people to be good stewards of the financial resources they possess.

TABLET #4:
Pyramid Of Prosperity

"Prosperity belongs to those who learn new things the fastest."

Paul Zane Pilzer

People learn things in different modalities. Some learn by vision, others by the ear. Some even learn through simulation. As I was developing the Gospel of Afronomics Theology, I had to learn what would be the most effective methods to teach this economic philosophy. One of the ways is through diagrams. The human mind thinks in pictures with vivid colors. I developed two diagrams as a means of how to apply the philosophy.

The first diagram is the Pyramid of Prosperity. The other is the Wealth Building Quadrant. These diagrams were designed for African people on the wealth-building journey. They can be used to measure where the wealth builder is in his sojourn.

The pyramid and the quadrant are intentionally done in color to emphasize the different phases of the wealth-building journey. Each color also represents an aspect of the African World Community and the flag of the UNIA led by the Honorable Right Excellent Marcus Garvey:

Red: (Blood of the African World Community) Over one billion people of African origin share the same blood. Regardless of whether it is on the African continent, the Caribbean, or Latin America

Black: (People of the African World Community) Reggae star Peter Tosh sang no matter where you are on the earth, if you're black, you are African! Khalid Abdul Muhammad said the Earth is our home and Africa is our throne.

Gold: (Wealth of the African World Community [e.g. mineral, financial, cultural]) Africa has been blessed with the mineral wealth that has built electronic empires such as SONY, Microsoft, Apple, and Dell.

Green: (Land of the African World Community) Africa has over one billion "children" across the globe. Africa has also been the "parent" of humanity and the "cradle" of civilization.

The pyramid consists of a three-phase process to wealth and prosperity. The pyramid is protected by a black border symbolizing a nucleus of culture, history, and spirituality. This pyramid is to reflect how wealth is to be acquired, earned, invested, protected, influenced, and bequeathed by African people.

BROTHER MINISTER ZUMBI Y. SHAWALA

PYRAMID OF PROSPERITY

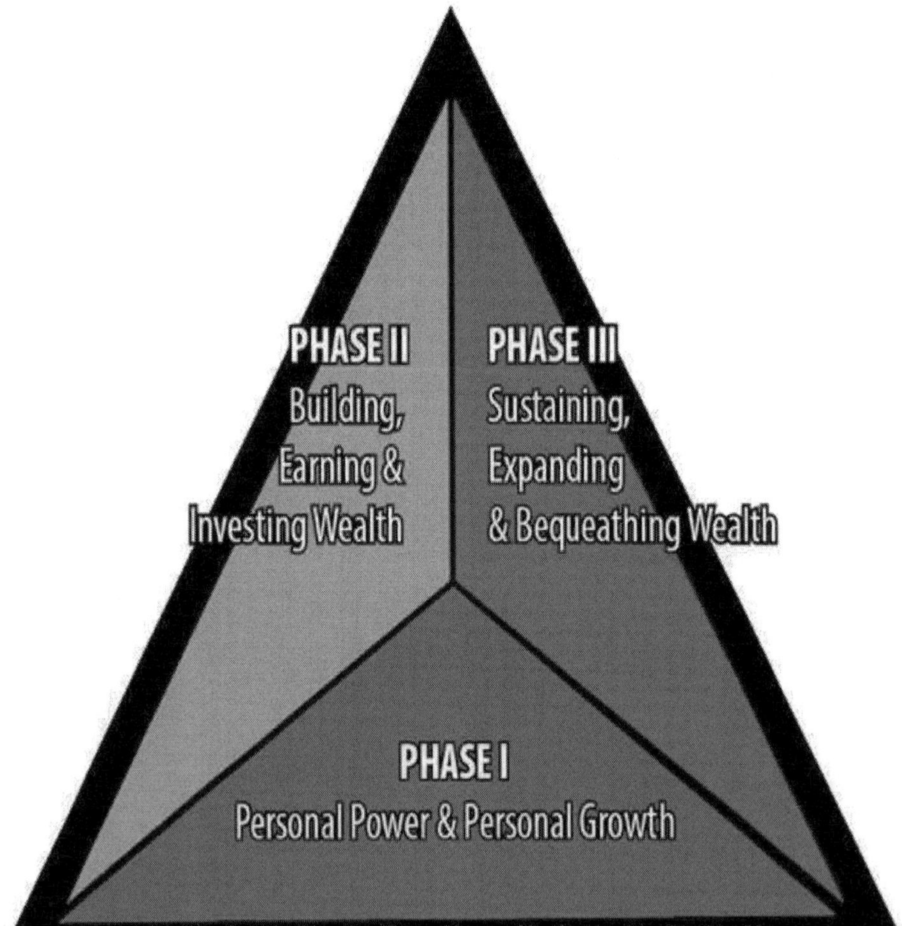

Phase 1 (Personal Power & Growth) (Red)

- **Objective**: Acquisition of Knowledge and Resources
- **Problem**: You don't know where to begin
- **Challenge**: Creating streams of income/revenue outside of a job
- **Opportunity**: Acquiring enough resources to put to work while obtaining the knowledge to manage and master money
- **Critical Skill(s) Needed**: 10% Solution, Raising Capital, Sales

Develop a plan to achieve the primary goal/objective of Phase I. What steps do I need to take to create a stream of income/revenue outside of a job? What skill sets do I need to learn to do it? How much does this stream need to generate to lead me towards financial freedom and economic independence? How much does this stream need to generate to use the profits to create a second stream outside of a job?

Phase II (Building, Earning & Investing Wealth) (Gold)

- **Objective**: Creating indestructible and multigenerational wealth
- **Problem**: Becoming financially free and economically independent of a job
- **Challenge**: Creating enough streams of income/revenue
- **Opportunity**: Solving the riddle of making money in your sleep (passive and residual income)
- **Critical Skill(s) Needed**: Building systems, putting money to work for you

Develop a plan to achieve the primary goal/objective of Phase 2. What steps are necessary to become financially independent of a job? How can I solve the riddle of making money in my sleep? How many streams of income/revenue will it take to be financially free of a job by age 40? How much does each stream need to generate to have a surplus of income to invest in purchasing income-generating assets?

Phase III (Sustaining, Expanding, Protecting & Bequeathing Wealth) (Green)

- **Objective:** Sustaining & Expanding the wealth built in Phases I and II
- **Problem:** Too much money
- **Challenge:** Protecting your wealth from "predators" (legal and illegal)
- **Opportunity:** Using Corporations, trusts, and other entities to create wealth building and wealth protection system(s)
- **Critical Skill(s) Needed:** Wealth protection, bequeathing wealth to the next generation

Develop a plan to achieve the primary goal/objective of Phase III. How do I expand and sustain the wealth I've built in Phases I and II? How do I begin protecting my wealth from "predators" (legal and illegal)? (e.g. family & friends, state & federal governments via taxes, banks, unions) How can corporations, trusts and other legal entities preserve and protect my wealth?

Border (Culture, History & Spirituality) (Black)

- **Objective:** Protecting the Economic Resources of African people
- **Problem:** Not operating on a "race first" paradigm
- **Challenge:** Operating unashamedly in the interests of African people
- **Opportunity:** Preparing future generations to create wealth through an African-centered paradigm
- **Critical Skill(s) Needed:** "Race First" consciousness

Develop a plan to achieve the primary goal/objective of the Border phase. What resources (tangible and intangible) do I bequeath to future generations and entities? Who have I mentored to create his/her wealth building and wealth protection systems? What nonprofit organizations will receive gifts from me after

I make my transition? Do I have a will in place? In what shape is my estate?

Each phase has its objectives, problems, challenges, and opportunities to lead the wealth builder into the next phase of the journey. To be successful, each phase requires a critical skill to achieve success. The border that protects the pyramid is the most critical. The accumulation of wealth, power, and resources is meaningless if the mindset of the wealth builder is not rooted in a nucleus of culture, history, and spirituality.

Proverbs 17:16 states "**Why pay tuition to educate a fool? For he has no intention of acquiring true wisdom**." (The Passion Translation) Phase I of the Pyramid of Prosperity reflects the wisdom of this passage. The first step in the wealth-building process is to acquire the necessary knowledge and information to build, sustain and bequeath wealth. Many times, there have been people who have come into a great windfall of money, only to lose it and be in a worse financial condition than before.

TABLET #5:

Wealth Building Quadrant

"The money you make is a symbol of the value you create."

- *Idowu Koyenikan*

In the previous chapter, I spoke of using diagrams to teach and apply the Gospel of Afronomics Theology. The second diagram is called the G.O.A.T. Wealth Building Quadrant. This quadrant is another guide for the wealth creator and wealth builder to measure his or her progress in the wealth-building sojourn. This quadrant is ideally made for those in the Generation Z generation because they can take advantage of all four quadrants. This quadrant is also reflective of a new and emerging economic paradigm based on shifts such as artificial intelligence, automation, robotics, globalization, outsourcing, downsizing, and privatization.

The quadrant is not a hard and fast rule. It is a guide to measure where the wealth builder is at, in his wealth-building journey. With the emergence of economic factors such as globalization, automation, and robotics, the G.O.A.T. Wealth Building Quadrant can be adjusted to fit one's personal circumstances. Like everything else in Nature, change is the only guaranteed constant.

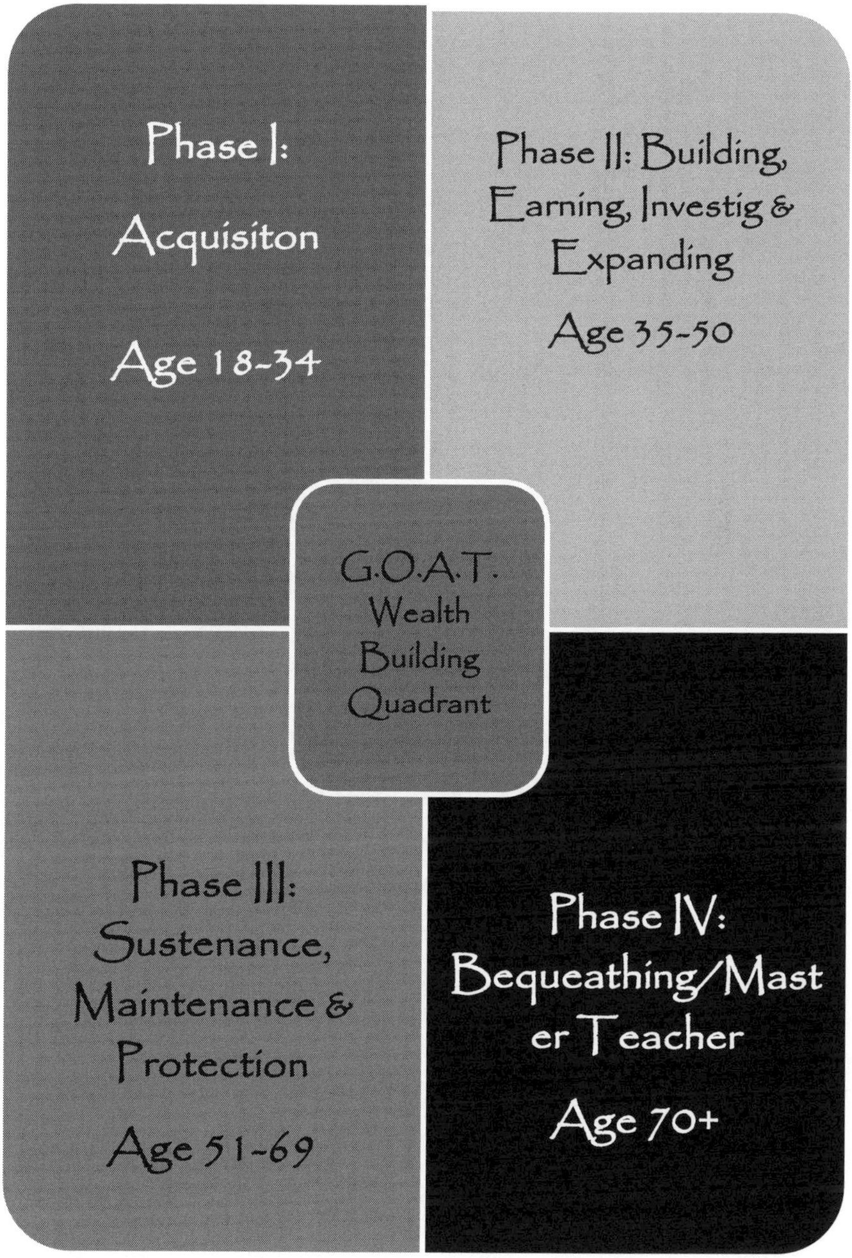
Phase I:
Acquisiton
Age 18-34
Phase II: Building, Earning, Investig & Expanding
Age 35-50
G.O.A.T. Wealth Building Quadrant
Phase III: Sustenance, Maintenance & Protection
Age 51-69
Phase IV: Bequeathing/Master Teacher
Age 70+

Phase I (Acquisition)

- **Age**: 18-34
- **Objective**: Acquisition of Resources
- **Problem**: You don't know where to begin

  Challenge: Creating a stream of income/revenue outside of a job
- **Opportunity**: Creating a second stream of revenue from the profits of the first stream
- **Net Worth Goal**: $5 million/$500,000 in monthly income/revenue

Develop a plan to achieve the primary goal/objective of Phase 1. What steps do I need to take to create a stream of income/revenue outside of a job? What skill sets do I need to learn to do it? How much does this stream need to generate to lead me towards financial independence? How much does this stream need to generate to use the profits to create a second stream outside of a job?

Phase II (Building, Earning & Investing Wealth)

- **Age**: 35-50
- **Objective**: Creating "mailbox money"
- **Problem**: Becoming financially free of a job
- **Challenge**: Creating enough streams of income/revenue
- **Opportunity**: Solving the riddle of making money in your sleep
- **Net Worth Goal**: $10 million/$1 million per month in income/revenue

Develop a plan to achieve the primary goal/objective of Phase 2. What steps are necessary to become financially independent of a job? How can I solve the riddle of making money in my sleep? How many streams of income/revenue will it take to be financially free of a job by age 40? How much does each stream need to generate to have a surplus of income to invest in purchasing income-generating assets?

Phase III (Sustaining & Expanding Wealth)

- **Age:** 51-69
- **Objective:** Sustaining & Expanding the wealth you built-in Phases 1&2
- **Problem:** Too much money
- **Challenge:** Protecting your wealth from "predators" (legal and illegal)
- **Opportunity:** Using Corporations, trusts, and other entities to create your wealth building and wealth protection system(s)
- **Net Worth Goal:** $ 10 Million+/$1 million+ in monthly revenue/income

Develop a plan to achieve the primary goal/objective of Phase 3. How do I expand and sustain the wealth I've built in Phases 1 and 2? How do I begin protecting my wealth from "predators" (legal and illegal)? (e.g. family & friends, state & federal governments via taxes, banks, unions) How can corporations, trusts and other legal entities preserve and protect my wealth?

Phase IV (Bequeathing)

- **Age:** 70+
- **Objective:** Bequeathing Wealth
- **Problem:** Determining who gets what
- **Challenge:** Finding Good Stewards
- **Opportunity:** Preparing future generations to create their own wealth building and wealth protection systems
- **Net Worth Goal: $** Infinite

Develop a plan to achieve the primary goal/objective of Phase 4. What resources (tangible and intangible) do I bequeath to future generations and entities? Who have I mentored to create his/her own wealth building and wealth protection systems? What nonprofit organizations will receive gifts from me after I make my transition? Do I have a will in place? In what shape is my estate?

TABLET #6:

G.O.A.T. Principles #1-10

G.O.A.T. Principle #1

We want African people to make a lifelong commitment to their personal development: By investing in personal development, African people can generate a return on **and** of investment (ROI) that is infinite. The late Jim Rohn stated that if you work hard on your job, you will make a living. If you work hard on yourself, you will make a fortune.

G.O.A.T. Principle #2

We want African people to create a clearly defined mission, vision, and purpose statement: In order to get from where you are to where you desire to be financial, you need to create a mission, vision, and purpose for your financial life. In your vision for your financial life, who do you aspire to be? In your mission statement, what is the purpose of the existence of your financial life? What do you intend to achieve or accomplish in your financial life? In your purpose statement, what is the purpose of the existence of your financial life? What is the driving force behind your financial life? These questions should help you develop an MVP statement that governs your business and financial life.

G.O.A.T. Principle #3

We want African people to invest 15-20 hours per week researching various wealth-creating and wealth-building opportunities: In our spare time, African people should be investing time in researching and experimenting with wealth-creating opportunities. We cannot afford to waste time engaged in activities that yield little to no economic fruit.

G.O.A.T. Principle #4

We want African people to invest 15-20 hours per week boosting their financial intelligence and financial IQ: African people need to sharpen and improve their financial IQ and financial intelligence in order to make intelligent money decisions, especially in the areas of investing, personal finance and understanding what a real asset is and what a real liability is.

G.O.A.T. Principle #5

We want African people to study and apply the business and financial philosophies of our "black titans" to their business and personal financial lives: Titans such as A.G. Gaston, S.B. Fuller,

Madame C.J. Walker and others have given us blueprints for economic prosperity. They not only became millionaires, multimillionaires and billionaires, but also injected a social responsibility to look after the affairs of their people.

G.O.A.T. Principle #6

We want African people to practice the 10% Solution (Pay Yourself First): African people need to treat themselves with the same or greater importance as any other bill they pay. W. Clement Stone states that this rule is the first rule to be mastered on the road to wealth and prosperity.

G.O.A.T. Principle #7

We want African people to (ideally) live on $.50- .60 of every dollar they earn: Along with practicing the 10% Solution, African people must (ideally) strive to live on $.50-.60 of every dollar they earn. By doing this, one can begin to discipline himself to incorporate this habit into his financial life and make it a priority. The Law of Magnetism states money goes where it is loved and respected. This habit is a demonstration of that love and respect.

G.O.A.T. Principle #8

We want African people to save and convert 30% of their annual salary into a stream of income beyond employment: African people need to create multiple streams of income in order to create the financial security and independence desired. African people should not be at the mercy of a paycheck, regardless of its size.

G.O.A.T. Principle #9

We want African people to develop, master, and monetize a financially valued skill (Sales, marketing, copyrighting, product development, raising capital, cashflow management): African people must develop a financially valued skill. If you work for someone, ask yourself how your position contributes to the company's bottom line. If you're a business owner, entrepreneur, or investor, you must focus on activities that generate income/revenue. Your value in the market increases when you can develop and master a skill that makes you a rainmaker.

G.O.A.T. Principle #10

We want African people to create a S.I.T.E.S. account (Storage, Investments, Tithing, Education, Startup Capital): African people can teach themselves and their children good money habits by establishing these accounts, which can even be something as simple as five jars.

G.O.A.T. Principles #11-20

TABLET #7:

G.O.A.T. Principles #11-20

G.O.A.T. Principle #11

We want African people to develop a monthly household budget and personal financial statement for each person in the household (Know Your Money): African people need to understand the importance of having an accurate, up-to-date personal financial statement. This habit will send a message to banks and other financial institutions that you are serious about your money and understand the importance of having a "positive imbalance".

G.O.A.T. Principle #12

We want African people to learn, master, and apply the skill of how to read financial statements (balance sheet, income/profit & loss statement,

cash flow statement): If African people are serious about building their business and financial empires, they must learn how to read financial statements (i.e., balance sheet, income statement, and cash flow statement). The numbers in financial statements tell a story to entrepreneurs, investors, and lenders. Financial statements give the lender a snapshot of the fiscal health of the company seeking financing. For investors, financial statements give them a picture of a company's profitability, management team, and how it manages its money. For entrepreneurs, financial statements help them understand financial reports and make sound business decisions.

G.O.A.T. Principle #13

We want African people to create and apply "Money Rules" to their personal and business financial lives: Everyone who is on the wealth-building trek has personal "money rules" that govern their financial lives. Whether it is how to save, how to invest, or how to protect it from financial "predators", all wealth-builders have a set of rules that govern their financial behavior.

G.O.A.T. Principle #14

We want African people to build a "cabinet" of wealth advisors (accountant, asset protection attorney, banker, certified financial planner, estate planning attorney, insurance agent, tax attorney, insurance agent/broker, real estate agent/broker, business advisor): Every wealth builder has "advisors to the King (or Queen)". A wealth builder has a team of experts to guide him in different aspects of business and personal finance. The team must have a clear understanding of what the wealth builder intends to achieve and accomplish so it can provide the "how" of achieving the objective(s).

From asset protection, estate planning, investing and tax strategies, the "cabinet" is led by the mission, vision, and purpose of the wealth builder. The team serves the wealth builder, not the other way around.

G.O.A.T. Principle #15

We want African people to build a Substantial Wealth Foundation: The road to financial independence begins with building a solid wealth foundation. Before the money comes, one must have the psychology, knowledge base, language, habits, and team established. Many times, people experience a significant windfall, only to eventually squander and waste it. They have an abundance of resources, yet lack the wisdom to manage and maximize them.

G.O.A.T. Principle #16

We want African people to know and master the Laws of Money: Money has laws that govern its usage. When you begin to understand how to make money your servant, you will thrive and prosper. Every dollar that comes through the wealth builder's hands must work harder than the wealth builder, especially if the wealth builder seeks to build multigenerational or "dynastic" wealth.

G.O.A.T. Principle #17

We want African people to create at least four streams of income per household: African people must understand the economic climate in which they live and operate. There was a time where a household could live from one stream of income. Now, even a two-income household is not enough. One of the income streams must produce residual income, or what is known as "mailbox money".

G.O.A.T. Principle #18

We want African people to create multiple streams of revenue in their business instead of building multiple businesses: African people must focus on building a strong business with multiple streams of revenue. The business must have a combination of product and service-based streams of revenue. There must also be residual and/or passive income so that the entrepreneur or business owner does not have to be present. The entrepreneur or business owner must solve the riddle of making money in his sleep for his business to grow and prosper. Only then can he take the profits from the business and put them to work for him through various investments.

G.O.A.T. Principle #19

We want African people to give 10% of their income to "race first" organizations committed to

improving the lives and livelihoods of African people: Charity begins at home, and African people need to consistently contribute to organizations that address our educational, cultural, spiritual and other civic needs.

G.O.A.T. Principle #20

We want African people to patronize black-owned businesses with 5-25% of their income: For African people to create their own economy, they must understand the importance of supporting their entrepreneurs and business owners that can provide similar services as their mainstream counterparts. By doing this, black entrepreneurs and business owners can build their own economic power base.

TABLET #8:

G.O.A.T. Principles #21-30

G.O.A.T. Principle #21

We want African people to practice "economic synergy" in their business lives: African people should create businesses that complement one another. Instead of competing for the same dollar, African people should find an industry or economy that can be complemented and supported.

G.O.A.T. Principle #22

We want African people to create susus in their homes and communities: There is a direct correlation of a people's trust, cultural cohesiveness, and economic prosperity. By creating "susus", or investment groups, we can learn the importance of collective work and responsibility, collective accountability, and sharing the fruits of their labor with each other.

G.O.A.T. Principle #23

We want African people to engage heavily in the manufacturing and distribution sectors of business: African people need to engage more in the production and distribution of products. Focusing on manufacturing and distribution will help African people acquire market share and attract their own talent from college(s). The real power and money and job creation come from the manufacturing and distribution sectors of business.

G.O.A.T. Principle #24

We want African people to create "new money" to eliminate old debts: You cannot budget your way out of debt. There needs to be an increase in your present revenue stream or create another stream of revenue. Also, you need a different kind of thinking to get you out of debt because your best thinking is what led you into the financial mess you created. How you choose to solve old debts is an indicator of your financial intelligence and financial IQ.

G.O.A.T. Principle #25

We want African people to build and sustain wealth BEFORE creating a lifestyle: The lifestyle you desire to experience can only be had after you've built the wealth necessary to sustain it. Many times, when we experience a windfall, we use these financial blessings to get bling as opposed to purchasing and creating income-generating assets that will pay for our lifestyle. "Business before pleasure" never rang more true than today. Money does not make you rich. It's what you think, say, and do that determines your prosperity or poverty. The book of Proverbs states the possession of money means nothing if you do not pursue the knowledge to manage and master it.

G.O.A.T. Principle #26

We want African people to improve their consumption-to-production ratio: For African people to experience true wealth, they must shift their mindset to increase production and reduce excess consumption. Black-owned businesses produce $1.00 for every $7.00-10.00 consumed by black customers. This is why I advocate for an entrepreneurial revolution amongst our people. We've proven brand loyalty and the ability to purchase high-priced ticket items. Now, we need to prove we can produce our own brands, products, and services.

G.O.A.T. Principle #27

We want African people to (ideally) achieve financial independence before or at age 40-50: To solve the riddle of financial independence, one must figure out how to make money in one's sleep. In building wealth, velocity becomes a huge factor. When you gain financial independence, what you've done is bought more time to live life on your terms. Your financial plan must consider velocity. Becoming financially independent requires a shift in priorities from job security to the "fast track". Choose the proper vehicles that radically increase your income.

G.O.A.T. Principle #28

We want African people to be and become business owners, entrepreneurs, and professional investors, NOT hustlers: If African people are serious about the resurrection of Black Wall Street and be a true economic force, then the focus must shift from being a "hustler" to being builders, creators, investors and maintainers of wealth. In many cases, hustlers never create an "exit strategy" because they have become addicted to "fast money". You may have to hustle to get, but hustling won't maintain the wealth you acquired over time.

G.O.A.T. Principle #29

We want African people to "Build Black" in order to "Buy Black": In order to support black-owned businesses, there must be black-owned businesses to support. "Building Black" not only means to build businesses but also by creating industries that African people can dominate. "Buying Black" leaves us at the retail level. "Building Black" raises us to a manufacturing and distribution level.

G.O.A.T. Principle #30

We want African people to form Mastermind groups: African people must learn to move as a team. Mastermind groups can serve as "think tanks" where entrepreneurs, business owners, and professional investors can exchange ideas, give support and hold one another accountable. No one has ever built wealth alone. Business and investing are team sports.

TABLET #9:

G.O.A.T. Principles #31-40

G.O.A.T. Principle #31

We want African people to create a "Freedom Fund": African people should create a Freedom Fund" account where each dollar deposited into that account is applied towards your financial freedom. We are ultimately responsible for bankrolling our economic liberation. Each day, you must ask yourself if you want your economic liberation or better treatment on the plantation. Having a Freedom Fund is a step in the direction of financial freedom and independence.

G.O.A.T. Principle #32

We want African people to keep a financial journal to document their wealth-building journey: If you choose to live an extraordinary life, you must be willing to record it. Keeping a journal allows you to chronicle your wealth-building and measure your progress and growth. It serves as a constant companion to place your thoughts and ideas. This journal can also serve as a "blueprint" for the next generation to guide them on their wealth-building journey.

G.O.A.T. Principle #33

We want African people to use the master-apprentice relationship model to teach future generations of business owners, entrepreneurs, and professional investors, NOT hustlers: African people need to begin grooming future generations to become the business owners, entrepreneurs, and professional investors necessary to build and maintain economic autonomy. We must recognize leadership potential in our youth as early as possible and begin laying the foundation. Train a child in the way he should go, and he will never depart from the path.

G.O.A.T. Principle #34

We want African people to work for royalties and dividends instead of a big check**:** In the Rich Dad philosophy, Robert Kiyosaki states the first rule is that the rich don't work for money. A more accurate statement is that the rich do not work for a paycheck. Part of the reason is that a paycheck is taxed at a higher rate than residual income. Also, residual income offers the potential for financial independence.

G.O.A.T. Principle #35

We want African people to teach and demonstrate to their children how to become producers through entrepreneurial ventures: Due to the shift in the global economy, the market is demanding that people become producers as opposed to consumers. African parents need to teach their children the importance of creating their economic opportunities, regardless of the state of the economy. Self-reliance and self-sufficiency are now the order of the day.

G.O.A.T. **Principle** *#36*

We want African people to become the #1 employer of African people: African people need to be in a position to employ their own people. The Honorable Elijah Muhammad stated the day will come when whites cannot even afford to employ their own people. That time is here, and we are still begging for entry into a burning house with no fire extinguisher.

G.O.A.T. Principle #37

We want African people to focus on building businesses that generate a minimum of $1-10 million in annual revenue: African people need to build businesses of significant size in order to not only compete but also to attract potential financiers and position themselves for joint ventures. This focus will also allow the opportunity to create jobs and careers for other people.

G.O.A.T. Principle #38

We want African people to create, grow, keep and bequeath the businesses they create to future generations of black business owners, entrepreneurs, and professional investors: African people cannot expect to build an economy of their own when their entrepreneurs and business owners continue to allow the "Great Black Buyout" by **FORTUNE 500** companies. How can we employ our own when we give away our companies for pennies on the dollar? It is our responsibility as entrepreneurs, business owners, and professional investors to create gainful employment with living wages for our people

G.O.A.T.* Principle #*39

We want African people to find potential mates who are fiscally responsible and emotionally mature: Money is an emotional subject, and to experience financial prosperity, one must become and find a potential mate who is fiscally responsible and emotionally mature. Many relationships have been destroyed because the individuals in the relationship/marriage have displayed emotional immaturity and fiscal irresponsibility. Each couple should take time out to create a financial mission, vision, and purpose statement so they can build a financial empire of their own.

G.O.A.T. Principle #40

We want African people to "mind their own business.": It is not the role of the government or your employer to make you rich and wealthy. That job is your responsibility. The job of your employer is to ensure you receive your payday check. The job of the government is to regulate a level playing field. The road to financial independence begins when you make your financial life a priority and take steps to build a financial empire of your own. The government and your employer know how to cover their fiduciary asses. It is your duty, obligation, and responsibility to cover yours as well.

TABLET #10:
G.O.A.T. Principles #41-50

G.O.A.T. Principle #41

We want African people to (ideally) generate an annual pre-tax income of $100,000 BEFORE starting a family: African people need to place themselves in the best possible position to raise a family. According to the USDA, if a couple has a child in 2000 or after, that child, over 20 years, is projected to cost the couple approximately $320,000-350,000. Also, adults with children are projected to stay an extra ten years in the workforce. When starting a family, we require long-term planning to be financially able to meet the needs of the child(ren). The couple must also consider inflation as a factor in starting a family.

G.O.A.T. Principle #42

We want African people to (ideally) save $10,000 for their unborn children: African people must give their children a fighting chance by starting their lives with $10,000. The minute the woman knows she's pregnant, there needs to be a fundraiser to make sure that child has $10,000 by the time s/he is born. There's no way we can build intergenerational wealth when we make each generation start from ground zero. Between the baby shower, crowdfunding, and personal savings, the child should have $10,000 ready to be placed in a trust, money market fund, or another investment vehicle.

G.O.A.T. Principle #43

We want African people to leave an economic legacy for future generations: As adults, the biggest crime we commit is making our youth start at ground zero every 20-30 years. While our counterparts receive the resources and knowledge to continue and expand wealth, we continue to give our youth nothing but the "I got mine, get yours!" lecture. I understand the importance of instilling a work ethic, but stop tying one arm behind their backs and expecting them to perform miracles with a handicap.

G.O.A.T. Principle #44

We want African people to develop an asset protection strategy: Financial predators are constantly looking for ways to separate you from your wealth. As a wealth builder, it is your responsibility to work with your team to create an asset security system. The three main topics involved in asset protection are tax reduction, protection from lawsuits, and estate and retirement planning.

G.O.A.T. Principle #45

We want African people to IMMEDIATELY begin estate planning: Everyone needs to begin estate planning, especially those who have a spouse and dependent(s). Estate planning is not just for the rich. Estate planning is for anyone who has assets they want to bequeath at the time of their transition. The ultimate objective is to transfer wealth to heirs and/or beneficiaries with as little taxation and complications as possible.

G.O.A.T. Principle #46

We want African people to "get your biz legit.": As wealth builders, African people must begin to legitimize their financial empire and have it documented. Things such as trusts, articles of incorporation, articles of organization (LLC's), living wills, and other documentation are necessary to protect assets and build estates to transfer assets to the next generation.

G.O.A.T. Principle #47

We want African people to keep a low profile about their wealth (Sutton's Law): In the movie **AMERICAN GANGSTER**, Frank Lucas warned his cousin Huey about dressing flamboyantly and attracting unwanted attention ("The loudest one in the room is the weakest one in the room"). As part of the wealth builder's asset protection plan, he must remember that silence is golden. The less the public knows about your wealth, the less likely you will become a target of financial "predators". The rich give to charities in silence. They build their wealth in silence. They bequeath their assets in silence. They practice what I call the "Black Hand Theory". The theory states that it is the people who are rarely seen, heard, or discussed who are the true shot callers, policymakers, and check writers. In the immortal words of KRS-ONE, "**REAL** bad boys move in silence!"

G.O.A.T. Principle #48

We want African people to know, understand and use tax codes to their advantage: Taxes are one of the biggest threats to destroying wealth. African people must learn to **LEGALLY** reduce taxes with the advice of a tax attorney who can guide the wealth builder through the complexities of tax codes. There are numerous tax strategies and deductions available to the wealth builder that can significantly reduce his tax bill. In building wealth, it's not how much you make, but how much you keep that matters.

G.O.A.T. Principle #49

We want African people to focus on building wealth instead of making money: For African people to build, maintain, protect, and bequeath their financial assets, they must focus on building wealth that lasts. Making money is the "easy" part. The challenge is to make the money work for you and outlive you. John D. Rockefeller, Sr is gone. Yet, his money continues to dictate policy all over the world. His wealth has shaped education, politics, medicine, and business.

G.O.A.T. Principle #50

We want African people to break and violate Parkinson's Law: Parkinson's Law states that expenses will rise to meet income. In some cases, those expenses can exceed income. African people must relentlessly violate and break this law by simultaneously reducing expenses and increasing income or revenue. By doing this, African people can experience a "positive imbalance" on their financial statements.

G.O.A.T. Principles #51-60

TABLET #11:

G.O.A.T. Principles #51-60

G.O.A.T. Principle #51

W*e want African people to develop their personal wealth building formula:* No two people achieve wealth the same way. Russell Simmons built his fortune through music and fashion. Cathy Hughes built her wealth through radio ownership. R. Don Peebles built his wealth through real estate development. There are many paths and many formulas to wealth building. Find a formula that works for you and follow that path until you become successful.

G.O.A.T. Principle #52

We want African people to build a personal business, financial and personal development library: Rich people have big libraries, while poor people have big-screen TVs. There is a direct correlation between the screen size of a television and the size of a person's library. How many books, CD's, DVD's, and home study courses are in our libraries? How many of us have converted our homes into miniature learning institutions? I agree with using the library to check out books and other materials. But, there's nothing like having your own learning arsenal at your disposal when you need it.

G.O.A.T. Principle #53

We want African people to "own assets" and rent liabilities: When Robert Kiyosaki stated that a home is not an asset, the financial industry called him everything but a child of God. Ten years after that statement was made, the housing bubble burst, and many people lost their homes. Owning a home is an emotional thing. However, from a cash flow perspective, the house is a liability. Homeownership no longer makes financial sense, especially if you're paying a mortgage on that house. The new mantra is to own assets and rent liabilities. Own assets that put money in your pocket and rent liabilities that take money out of your pocket.

G.O.A.T. Principle #54

We want African people to "Pay your motherf&%@ing freedom dues: Everything in Nature has a price tag, and having wealth is no different. Malcolm's response to a reporter's question about what price must African people pay for freedom: "The price of freedom is death". Not only physical death but also a death of lack, security, and poverty consciousness. African people must "kill" the poverty consciousness and pay the price for financial freedom. Those who choose security over freedom deserve neither.

G.O.A.T. Principle #55

We want African people to create a sense of community as part of a sound black economic blueprint for the 21st century and beyond: Part of a people's economic prosperity lies in its ability to create a sense of community amongst itself. A community does not necessarily require occupying a particular physical space but having a collective mindset committed to a core set of beliefs and values. For example, there are over two billion Muslims globally. Yet, they subscribe to the Five Pillars. In regards to economic development, a community can be formed by resolving the economic needs and issues of a group of people.

G.O.A.T. Principle #56

We want African people to produce 1000 culturally conscious millionaires, multimillionaires, and billionaires per year over a ten-year period: African people are at a critical point in time where they can no longer rely on millionaires, multimillionaires, and billionaires (inside or outside the race) to assist them in transcending poverty and bringing prosperity to themselves. In other words, African people must produce the kind of millionaires, multimillionaires, and billionaires necessary. African people are wasting time criticizing athletes, entertainers, and others for not making financial contributions to "race first" causes. If African people are as great as they say they are, then all they need is their self-reliance and spirituality. The source of all substance lies in the Universe, not man. Man is just a delivery service.

G.O.A.T. Principle #57

We want African people to build "indestructible wealth.": Indestructible wealth is wealth that can withstand any financial turbulence that occurs (e.g., recession, depression, etc.). Wealth should be invested in things people need, regardless of the state of the economy. For example, investing in laundromats can create indestructible wealth because people need to do laundry.

G.O.A.T. Principle #58

We want African people to set and achieve the goal of creating a personal net worth of at least $10 million: African people must be aware of the rate of inflation and other factors that can adversely impact their capacity to build wealth. Since the creation of the Federal Reserve in 1914, the US dollar has lost over 97% of its purchasing power. The devaluing of the US dollar was accelerated in

1933 when President Franklin D. Roosevelt cut ties with the gold standard to allow the government to pump more money into the US economy and stimulate it. In 1971, Richard Nixon suspended the practice of foreign nations to sap US gold reserves, bringing the US into a fiat economy.

G.O.A.T. Principle #59

We want African people to live a vision-oriented business and financial life: The aspiring wealth builder must live a vision-based financial life instead of a condition-based financial life. Every millionaire, multimillionaire, and billionaire had to answer the question "Who do I aspire to be as a wealth builder?". In many cases, money was not the driving force; wealth-builders were driven by a desire to change the world. Wealth builders are visionaries who see the world with the mind, not the eye. Albert Einstein said it best: Imagination is greater than intelligence.

G.O.A.T. Principle #60

We want African to realize they have an income (cashflow) problem, not a budgeting problem: Conventional financial wisdom teaches that one must control spending in order to become wealthy. Not true. The issue has always been "income, income, income". You cannot cost-cut your way to prosperity and profitability, be it personal or business.

Advisors to the King (Or Queen)

TABLET #12:

Advisors to the King (Or Queen)

"A fool despises good counsel, but a wise man takes it to heart."

Confucious

"Move as a team

Never move alone

Or welcome to the Terrordome"

Public Enemy

"Welcome to the Terrordome"

From **FEAR OF A BLACK PLANET** *(1990)*

The concept of the "self-made millionaire" is the biggest lie ever perpetrated in the history of business. No titan has singlehandedly built his fortune as a solo act. Wealth creation and wealth-building are the results of a total team effort. I have a saying: it takes courage to create and build wealth; but it takes intelligence to manage, maintain and protect wealth. And that requires a well-skilled team committed to a single cause.

Every wealth creator and builder must build a team of experts in specific areas of business, personal finance, real estate, and taxes. In my years of research and discussions with successful wealth builders, there are ten positions that are the foundation of a wealth builder's "cabinet" of advisors:

1. **Accountant/CPA**: This position is to help the wealth builder in specific issues involving structuring your finances, understanding tax laws, and establish the proper legal entities to protect your assets. The accountant can also help in developing a personal financial statement to determine the net worth of the wealth builder and what areas need improvement.
2. **Attorney/Lawyer**: This position is to help the wealth builder review and interpret contracts, advise and represent clients in court, before government agencies and private legal matters and interpret laws, rules, and regulations for individuals and businesses.
3. **Banker (Personal/Investment)**: Personal bankers usually work in retail banking branches to assist clients with various banking and financial needs. Investment bankers

4. **CFP/Financial Advisor**: This position works in not only budgeting but developing a comprehensive financial plan for the wealth builder. The financial planner/advisor primarily helps the wealth builder with investing and achieving specific financial goals.
5. **Insurance Agent/Broker**: This position involves the selling and negotiating of health, life, property, or another type of insurances to meet the needs of their clients. The wealth builder needs to ensure his family and physical assets are protected
6. **Estate Planning Attorney**: This position involves helping clients determine the specific distribution of their estate, provide those seeking to establish trusts where assets are set aside for a future beneficiary, and drafting wills, trusts, and other estate planning documents.

7. **Asset Protection Attorney**: This position includes helping clients find legal ways to protect their assets when lawsuits, bankruptcy, creditor claims, or other liabilities arise. They can discuss the advantages and disadvantages of certain asset protection tools (e.g. corporate structures, asset protection trusts, and retirement plans) with their clients.
8. **Tax Attorney**: This position involves understanding finance and accounting principles, keeping confidential records and tax information for clients and ensuring compliance with all IRS deadlines, and coordinate with clients to file all tax returns.
9. **Real Estate Agent/Broker**: This position involves helping the client, buy, sell or rent residential and commercial properties.
10. **Business Advisor/Coach**: The business advisor must share similar values as the wealth builder.

He will help in identifying goals, develop business models and plans, assist in raising capital possess a coaching mentality.

Wealth Building Cabinet

Develop a plan to achieve the primary goal/objective of building a wealth-building cabinet. What steps are necessary to fulfill each position in the cabinet? How do I find the right people? Can I find referrals or recommendations? What criterion do I need to use to interview potential candidates? Do I have a clearly defined mission, vision, and purpose for building wealth?

In Napoleon Hill's **THINK AND GROW RICH**, Hill talks of the importance of the "Master Mind". In order to achieve financial freedom and economic independence, one must organize and align himself with great minds that were experts in their respective fields. Henry Ford started the most difficult job a leader has is to keep two or more people focused on the same goal and driven by the same mission, vision, and purpose.

Ford also knew he did not have the time, energy, or patience to learn everything about the business. So, he assembled the greatest minds in finance, engineering, sales, marketing, and accounting. Ford had to know enough about a little bit of each subject to have an intelligent conversation with his specialists. Ford understood the power and importance of a team in achieving great wealth, abundance, and prosperity.

G.O.A.T.
Wealth Building Cabinet

Accountant/CPA: ______________________________

Attorney/Lawyer:

____

Banker:

____

CFP/Financial Advisor:

____

Insurance Agent/Broker:

____

Estate Planning Attorney:

____

Asset Protection Attorney:

____

Tax Attorney:

____

Real Estate Agent/Broker:

____

Business Advisor(s)/Consultant(s)/Coach:

____

____

____

Notes:

____

____

____

____

____

____

____

____

Notes:

TABLET #13:

Multiple Streams Of Income For African-Centered Millionaires

If you have a million-dollar problem, can it be solved with a $50,000 job? More importantly, are you using the proper vehicles to resolve this financial issue?

I remember the comedy series **IN LIVING COLOR** from the early 1990's. There was a skit called, "Hey, Mon!". The skit focuses on a Jamaican family where each individual has multiple jobs. One brags about having two jobs, while another family member boasts of having three jobs. Although the skit was funny and satirical, it exposes a fundamental flaw in how African people have chosen to solve their financial problems. This is not an indictment because they only did what they knew. However, when you know better, you do better.

When studying the rich, African people will find that the millionaires, multimillionaires, and billionaires do not rely on a single source of income. Nor do they rely on "active income", or income that is only earned when performing a job or rendering service as a self-employed individual.

Rich people create multiple streams of income and have figured out ways to make money in their sleep. As potential wealth creators and wealth builders, African people must evolve beyond the 9-5 mentality and begin to "leverage" themselves. Having multiple jobs does not equal multiple streams of income because each job requires a specific amount of time. In the immortal words of Bobby Byrd, "If you don't work, then you don't eat!"

In the wealth-building journey, African people must create multiple streams of income. There are seven specific income streams that rich people use to build and maintain wealth:

1. **Earned Income**: This income stream is the result of generating income through a job or performing a service as a self-employed

individual. This is trading time for money, which is never an equal exchange.

2. **Rental Income**: This income stream is the result of receiving rent from an asset you own (e.g. residential and/or commercial real estate).
3. **Interest Income**: This income stream is the result of lending money to an individual, business, or other commercial entity. Lending can include investing money in a microloan program, purchasing Treasury Bills, or Savings Bonds.
4. **Profit Income**: This income stream is the result of buying wholesale and selling retail. Profit income is generated through entrepreneurship or business-to-business (B2B) sales as a manufacturer and/or distributor.

5. **Royalty Income**: This income stream is the result of others paying you for use of your intellectual property (e.g. logos, songs, sheet music, etc.).
6. **Capital Gains**: This income stream is the result of an asset's increase in value.
7. **Dividend Income**: This income stream is the result of making money from shares of stock in publicly traded companies.

These income streams are necessary for the wealth builder to achieve financial freedom and economic independence. The recent outbreak of COVID-19 has exposed those who have relied on one or two streams of income and reinforces the importance of not only having multiple streams of income but also having income streams that are automated.

For example, one can use either Gumroad (**www.gumroad.com**) or Payhip (**www.payhip.com**) to set up a membership or subscription that can generate income at the first of each month. Imagine having 200 subscribers paying you a monthly subscription fee of $100. That's $20,000 that required no work!

So, let's solve this riddle of making money in our sleep so we can have the financial freedom and economic independence to live life on our terms.

Multiple Streams of Income (MSI)

Tom Corley, the author of **RICH HABITS**, did a five-year study of rich people and their characteristics. During his study, Corley discovered the following:

- 65% of self-made millionaires had three streams of income

- 45% of self-made millionaires had four streams of income
- 29% of self-made millionaires had five streams of income

Corley's study reveals the importance of creating multiple streams of income to achieve financial freedom and economic independence. It also exposes the need for some or all income streams to generate passive and residual income. Warren Buffett said the key to financial freedom is solving the riddle of making money in your sleep. If you do not solve this riddle, then you will work for money all the days of your life.

Develop your MSI Plan

Develop a plan to achieve the primary goal/objective of having multiple streams of income. What steps are necessary to become financially free and economically independent through multiple streams of income? How can I solve the riddle of making money in my sleep? How many streams of income/revenue will it take to be financially free of a job by age 40? How much does each stream need to generate to have a surplus of income to invest in purchasing income-generating assets (IGA's)?

Earned Income:

____

____

____

____

____

____

____

____

____

Rental Income:

Interest Income:

Profit Income:

Royalty Income:

Capital Gains:

Dividend Income:

As you develop your MSI Plan, think of the benefits that multiple streams of income can bring to your financial life. An August 12, 2020 post of Middlechase Blog, gives the following benefits of having Multiple Streams of Income:

1. **Less Risk, Greater Control**: Having multiple streams of income protects you from financial risk. It also gives you greater control over your financial life.

2. **Financial protection against job insecurity**: With the rise of artificial intelligence and automation, having multiple streams of income protects you from the psychological and emotional trauma one can suffer from loss of employment.

3. **Early Retirement**: Having multiple streams of income can accelerate your ability to earn, save and invest more money into high-yield investment vehicles.

4. **Build Long-Term Wealth**: Having passive income streams today can lead to less work in the future. A sound wealth building system will consist of multiple streams of income that can generate infinite passive income.

5. **Create Room to generate more money**: When you have multiple streams of income, you can reach financial freedom and economic independence faster. Ecclesiastes 11:1-6 even teaches the importance of having multiple streams of income.

Warren Buffett stated the outbreak of COVID-19 has exposed those who have been "swimming naked". Living on one stream of income places an individual in a dangerously vulnerable position. Many people have suffered job losses, businesses lost to government-mandated shutdowns and an economy that is transforming through artificial intelligence, automation, robotics, globalization, privatization, downsizing, and outsourcing.

All wealth builders understand that financial freedom and economic independence will not come from one stream of revenue. The more streams of revenue you have, the greater chance you will achieve your financial goals at a faster rate.

Get Your Biz Legit

TABLET #14:

Get Your Biz Legit

Many of us claim to be "handling our business" or "taking care of business." Yet, the business we claim to have doesn't generate any revenue. Therefore, your "business" is nothing but a hobby. To be taken seriously, you must get your business in order. That means separating your assets from the business assets. I can show people the process of how to legitimize their business for $1000 or less:

Get a free phone number through Google Hangouts Dialer to use as a business phone number

1. Get business address through UPS or post office
2. Incorporate your business as an LLC or Subchapter S corporation

3. Get EIN# through IRS (**www.irs.gov**)
4. Open a **business** bank account
5. Get DUNS# (**www.dnb.com**)
6. Open an online payment account (PayPal, WePay, Stripe, etc.)
7. Get a domain name (GoDaddy, Host Gator, Namecheap, etc.)
8. Create a website (GoDaddy, WordPress, Wix, Weebly, etc.)
9. Order business cards through **STAPLES** (**www.design.staples.com/category/business-cards**)
10. Open a **free** account with Wave Accounting (**www.waveapps.com**) for your accounting/ bookkeeping needs

The biggest expense will be filing your Articles of Incorporation or Articles of Organization for a limited liability company (LLC) with your state of residence.

Half of the steps taken are free of charge. However, I do recommend that you do these steps to make sure you execute the entire plan.

I do not recommend a DBA Sole Proprietorship or Partnership. The business world will not take you seriously nor recognize you as a legitimate business. Plus, you cannot protect your assets from a potential lawsuit or other creditors who seek to seize your assets. There must be a complete separation and establish a separate entity to conduct business. In most cases, the entity of choice is either an LLC or Subchapter S corporation. By using these entities, you have a better chance of raising capital via selling shares.

In the wealth-building process, one must build an infrastructure to handle the money as it comes through your business. Using entities such as corporations are necessary to protect your personal and business assets. In a lawsuit-happy society, asset protection is a must.

TABLET #15:

The S.C.R.I.B.E. Of the G.O.A.T.

When Napoleon Hill accepted the challenge of documenting the secrets of personal achievement and success from Andrew Carnegie, he embarked upon a path of becoming a scribe to chronicle what became the Science of Personal Achievement. In 1998, I began a journey of developing a black economic liberation theology for African people that will eventually outlive me. Just as **THINK AND GROW RICH** continues to influence millions since 1937, I intend to have G.O.A.T. continue to influence and impact African people in the 21st century and beyond.

As a "scribe" of G.O.A.T., I decided to create, a truly diversified portfolio that would be for African people. When people hear "diversify", they think it means to buy different things within one type of asset. For example, people will purchase different types of mutual funds, thinking they are diversifying their portfolio. Real diversification can only happen **AFTER** one has focused on earning and radically increasing his income or revenue.

Real asset diversification is what I call "**S.C.R.I.B.E.**". **S.C.R.I.B.E.** is an anacronym I developed that I feel is a comprehensive portfolio for African people. S.C.R.I.B.E. will help African people develop the multigenerational wealth necessary to resolve the economic issues confronting African people domestically and globally. S.C.R.I.B.E. stands for:

S - System(s)

C - Commodities

R - Real Estate

I - Investment(s) (Paper Assets)

B - Businesses

E - Employee Stock Ownership Plan (ESOP's)

This is a combination of creating and/or acquiring IGA's (income-generating assets), having a passive and residual income, and developing systems that not produce wealth, but also protect it. When you have this portfolio in place. You will go a long way towards financial freedom and economic independence.

S=System(s)

The human body is a system comprised of various systems, working in harmony and synergy towards a common objective: optimal health. When building wealth, everything begins with building an effective system that can not only produce wealth but protect it. Michael Gerber, the author of **THE E-MYTH REVISITED**, speaks of creating a "franchise prototype" business that can produce a pleasantly consistent (or consistently pleasant) result. He also speaks of building a system around the product or service to standardize the quality to guarantee the consistency of quality.

The aspiring wealth builder must think of building two systems: a wealth-producing system and a wealth protection system. The wealth-producing (or wealth building) system is designed to radically generate infinite income or revenue. The wealth protection system is designed to protect the IGA's (income-generating assets) and the wealth they generate. Corporations and trusts are the main vehicles used to secure assets and income.

C = Commodities

Commodities are basic goods used in commerce that is interchangeable with other goods of the same type. Commodities are commonly used as inputs in the production of other goods and services.

Commodities can be classified into one of three categories:

1. **Soft Commodities**: These are commodities that are grown, such as wheat and rice
2. **Hard Commodities**: These are commodities that are mined, such as gold, silver, and oil.
3. **Energy Commodities**: Examples include oil, electricity, gas, and coal.

There are two ways to invest in commodities:

1. Invest through exchange-traded funds (ETF's) that invest in commodity futures
2. Purchase the stocks and bonds of commodity producers (e.g. Mobil Exxon)

Many financial advisors recommend that an individual's portfolio should be 5-10% in commodities. Bullish financial advisors suggest up to 25% of a portfolio. Check with either a financial advisor or CFP (certified financial planner) to see what fits your situation in regards to incorporating commodities into your wealth-building strategy.

R = Real Estate

Real estate is a critical component in building multigenerational wealth. The power of real estate cannot be overestimated. When you study the portfolios of the rich and wealthy, real estate is the anchor of their wealth, especially real estate that generates infinite income.

The biggest landlord on Earth is McDonald's, followed by the Catholic Church.

What McDonald's learned is that by owning the land underneath the restaurant, they can build another stream of income into its revenue model.

So, McDonald's created its real estate division called the Franchise Realty Corporation. Its objective is to purchase prime real estate and own the land and building while leasing the land to the franchisee.

Ray Kroc, the founder of McDonald's, asked a group of business students at the University of Texas to guess what his business was. The answers varied from "restaurants", "hamburgers" and "fast food". He finally answered that his business was real estate. When potential franchisees attend "Hamburger U", which is located at McDonald's headquarters outside Chicago, there is a sign at the front desk that reads "Our business is real estate". McDonald's understands the importance of real estate in its revenue model.

I = Investments (Paper Assets)

When people hear "investments", they mostly think of purchasing shares of stock in a publicly-traded company. Investopedia defines an investment as "an asset or item acquired to generate income or appreciation" over time. In regards to paper assets (stocks, bonds, ETF's, etc.), many people invest for increased long-term value and consistent positive cash flow.

The one thing that must be understood is to avoid making the mistake of confusing speculation with investing. Investing is the intent of purchasing assets to build long-term wealth and positive cash flow, as opposed to speculation. Speculation is the process of attempting to capitalize on market inefficiencies for short-term profit. Speculation carries a greater risk than investing because of market volatility. Some financial experts have made speculating analogous to gambling.

One advantage of having investments in an individual portfolio is that portfolio income is taxed at a lower rate than earned income. Portfolio income is usually taxed at 20%

B = Businesses

Entrepreneurship has been a popular vehicle for building lasting wealth. Every October, **FORBES** magazine releases its annual **FORBES 400**. This list is comprised of the 400 richest people in America. A great percentage of these individuals made their fortunes through building businesses.

For example, Atlanta Falcons owner Arthur Blank made his fortune by building **THE HOME DEPT** with his partner and co-founder Bernie Marcus. Ted Turner built his financial empire by becoming a media mogul and owner of major League Baseball's Atlanta Braves. He is responsible for networks such as Turner Classic, TNT, CNN, Headline News, and TBS. Daymond John, the author of **RISE AND GRIND** and a regular on **SHARK TANK**, made his money through the creation of **FUBU** (For Us By Us), a clothing line for hip-hop and urban communities.

Building a business can benefit the wealth builder for the short and long term. The short-term benefit of building a business is to use the income to finance other ventures. The long-term benefits include an exponential increase in income, potential passive income, and increased value. One can build a business to the point where it becomes the product and can be sold as an asset (e.g. franchising).

A major mistake that aspiring entrepreneurs make is to "follow your passion". The problem with that philosophy is that there is little to no focus on solving problems in the market. The challenge is discovering if your passion can solve problems in the market. Successful entrepreneurs are driven by solving problems. Can your product, service, or business help the customer? Following your passion can be viewed as a selfish reason to go into business.

Wayne Huizenga, the founder of **WASTE MANAGEMENT, BLOCKBUSTER VIDEO,** and former owner of the NFL's Miami Dolphins, was being interviewed by a journalist for **ENTREPRENEUR** magazine. The journalist was asking Huizenga about being in the trash industry, home video industry, and other ventures. He asked Huizenga what is his business. Huizenga's response: "Son, I'm in the moneymaking business!"

The bottom line: If you are going to "follow your passion" you must create a product, service, or company that not only helps the customer but also can be scaled to generate big revenue. In today's economic climate, you must solve the riddle of:

1. Build a $1 million business over a 3-to-5-year period

2. Scale that business to a minimum of $10 million in annual revenue

Entrepreneurship is a vehicle that can provide the aspiring wealth builder with financial freedom and economic independence. Unlike other things that take time, require large amounts of capital, and have higher barriers to entry, entrepreneurship can put you on the fast track to wealth. With the internet, one can be in business with very little startup capital and no barrier of entry into the business arena.

E = Employee Stock Ownership Plan

An employee stock ownership plan (ESOP) is an employee benefit plan intended to encourage employees to acquire ownership (stocks) in the company. According to the National Center for Employee Ownership, approximately 6600 employee stock ownership plans are covering more than 14 million employees. Companies that are majority-owned employee companies include Publix Supermarkets, WinCo Foods, Farmers Home Furniture, Price Cutter Supermarkets, and Thrifty White Pharmacy. These companies are at least 50% owned by an ESOP.

ESOP's work like this: A company sets up a trust fund for employees and contributes either cash to purchase company stock, contribute shares directly to the planner or have the planner borrow money to purchase shares. Contributions made by the employee are tax-deductible. The employee contributes pre-tax income to the ESOP and only pax taxes when they receive stock when they leave or retire.

Participation in a company's ESOP has great benefits for the employee. According to a 1997 study conducted by Washington State, employees made 5-12% more in wages and triple the retirement assets as non-ESOP companies.

An ESOP can be a stream of income that can grow into a lucrative asset. While the employee receives a paycheck, he is also gaining equity in the company. One can say the employee is working for himself. It can go a long way to establishing the groundwork for multigenerational wealth.

Conclusion: Buffett vs Dalio

Warren Buffett and Ray Dalio are two of the world's top investors with opposing views on investing. Buffett believes in "focus", while Dalio favors "diversification". Real asset diversification requires both a focus and a diversification, using one stream of income to bankroll another stream of income.

Diversification only comes after focusing on earning revenue. The rich did not use diversification to build their fortunes. They used a laser-like focus on their venture. Once they earned a significant amount of revenue, they took those earnings and "put them to work". In **RICH DAD'S GUIDE TO INVESTING**, Robert Kiyosaki speaks of converting earned income (focus) into a portfolio and passive income (diversification).

For African people, the S.C.R.I.B.E. method of asset diversification can be a gamechanger in the wealth-building journey. To diversify, focus on building your financial empire. Generate significant income and revenue. Then, that those profits and convert them onto the other areas of S.C.R.I.B.E.

G.O.A.T. Ten-Point Tax Return Plan

TABLET #16:

G.O.A.T. Ten-Point Tax Return Plan

Note: I developed this plan in October 2019 and introduced it at a local Kwanzaa event on Day 4 (Ujamaa: Cooperative Economics). This was a few months before the COVID-19 pandemic of 2020. I wrote this to give African people a guide for their annual windfall of the tax refund. I never realized this same strategy could be used for the first set of stimulus checks issued in the spring of 2020. Money must always be your servant, not your master.

I firmly believe in creating a "plan" for your money. One of the biggest reasons is to protect you from your own emotions. Saying that money is an emotional subject is an understatement. Allowing your emotions to govern your financial affairs will lead you to financial destruction. Proverbs 17:16 (NIV) teaches "Why should fools have money in hand to buy wisdom when they are not able to understand it?" Getting paper is only part of the equation. Learning to manage and master money separates the rich from the poor.

1. **Gratitude**: African people must show gratitude for receiving this windfall. Call on the Universe and the ancestors for wisdom and guidance in handling such a windfall.
2. **Savings**: African people must practice the 10% Solution (Pay Yourself FIRST!) African people must save with a purpose (S.W.A.P.) and find an asset that can generate infinite passive income.
3. **Investment(s)**: African people must invest in income-generating assets that produce passive

income. African people must know how to convert earned income into a portfolio and passive income.

4. **Cultural Tithing**: African people must practice "cultural tithing" to a "race first" organization, regardless of one's spiritual school of thought. That organization must be committed to improving the (economic) condition of African people.
5. **Education**: African people must invest in an education comprised of entrepreneurship, financial literacy, personal development, and cultural consciousness. The core of our economic philosophy must be rooted in culture, history, and spirituality.
6. **Startup Capital**: African people must allocate a portion of their tax refund towards startup capital for a home-based/internet-based business.

7. **Pantry**: African people must build a pantry that can sustain a household (ideally) for up to one year. African people must stay prepared for any emergency that can arise.
8. **Petty Cash**: African people must have a "petty cash" fund in their households. Regardless of the amount, petty cash must be available to handle unexpected events.
9. **Insurance:** African people must have insurance as part of an estate planning and asset protection strategy. A basic life insurance plan can serve as a starting point of an estate planning strategy.
10. **Debt Reduction:** African people must reduce or eliminate as much consumer debt as possible, especially credit cards with high-interest rates.

This plan is to help you organize and maximize your refund (and/or stimulus check). When you plan and organize, you are taking control of your financial fate and destiny. Anytime you receive a windfall, there should be a plan in place to put the windfall to good use.

Another reason to have a plan for your money is to protect you from your emotions. Money is an emotional subject, and one must **NEVER** underestimate the impact money has on one's emotional intelligence (EQ). Emotional intelligence is 25 times more powerful than mental intelligence. A plan helps keep your emotions in check. A plan helps you stay on track with your financial goals and objectives. Use this plan as a springboard towards financial freedom and economic independence.

REPUBLIC OF NEW PALMARES MOVEMENT

When in the course of human events, a people find themselves in a predicament where it cannot produce, provide for or protect itself, that people must choose to be free or suffer the consequences of what that dependency on other groups of people will be: **DEATH**! When a people must rely on other races for their goods, services, and provision, that race is an economic and political slave.

When African people stand at the crossroads of their economic freedom, they are in a similar predicament as the Israelites of the Torah, Bible, and Quran. We have been given "great substance" to the tune of over $2 trillion in purchasing power. Yet, with as much great substance as we have, we lack the wisdom and knowledge to apply it for our benefit.

Can I prove it? Yes! How can we have over $2 trillion in our hands, yet learn that 44% of America's homeless are African people and 52% of America's homeless are African families? Why do we have such a disproportionate number of African women being forced to seek provision from welfare agencies and social service programs? Why are there so few black-owned businesses consistently generating over $10 million in annual revenue? Why are our college students buried under tremendous amounts of debt and grossly underemployed or unemployed?

These are some of the questions that our economists, policymakers, and others who are for the upliftment of African people need to ask and answer. As a self-proclaimed "Afronomicist" and "Afrofuturist", I seek answers to these questions and have developed possible solutions.

One of my solutions is the **GOSPEL OF AFRONOMICS THEOLOGY**. This philosophy is a 60-point program with 16 Core Beliefs and "Ten Commandments" that can allow African people to take control of their destiny at a personal and collective level. It offers African people a fighting chance to become financially free and independent. Financial freedom is a form of consciousness, while economic independence is having the resources to take advantage of one's financial freedom.

The reason I start with financial freedom first is to examine where we are as a people. There is a global economy of over $300 trillion. Over $1.4 trillion circles the planet every 24 hours. In America, the national GDP (gross domestic product) is USD 19.75 trillion. The purchasing power of African people in America is approximately $2 trillion as of 2020.

The troubling part is that for every dollar that enters African communities, $.98 leaves. It doesn't have a chance to reproduce itself amongst us. Also, 98% of African people work for non-African people or entities. Therefore, how can we, in good conscience, shout "Nation Time!" when many of us are unwilling and/or unable to invest, even on a part-time basis, the necessary time, energy, and resources to build a reality of our own?

I have to seriously question our people's sincerity, integrity, character, and commitment when we preach the gospel of financial freedom and economic independence yet refuse to take even those baby steps to be free. That's not due to a lack of resources, but a lack of courage and confidence in one's mission, vision, and purpose.

What "baby steps" can we as a people take? First, you must decide and commit to your economic liberation. You must commit and practice to pay yourself **FIRST** through the 10% Solution. You must know that you have a right to a portion of your earnings. You must commit to supporting black-owned businesses with 5-25% of your income. Every dollar invested in a black-owned business is a dollar invested in building a black economy. This will require black customers and clients to make a conscious shift to a "race first" philosophy. There should be an all-out effort to allow our entrepreneurs and business owners to provide the best possible quality in goods and services to the marketplace.

My other solution is the Republic of New Palmares Movement. In the tradition of our independent enclaves like Durham (NC), Rosewood (FL) and Tulsa's (OK) famous "Black Wall Street", the Republic of New Palmares is a concept of creating African-owned and African-controlled quilombos that are self-sufficient and interdependent.

Each quilombo will practice what I call "economic synergy". Economic synergy means the businesses within a community should complement each other, as opposed to competing against each other. Each Republic of New Palmares will create a code of conduct that governs and defines appropriate and inappropriate conduct and how that behavior will be rewarded and punished.

The concept of the Republic of New Palmeres Movement comes from the freedom movement in Brazil where enslaved Africans escaped from the Portuguese and Dutch plantations to create their own communities called quilombos, loosely translated as "war camp" in Bantu. Its leader, Zumbi, was born free in 1655. He was kidnapped at age six by Portuguese slave raiders and raised by a missionary priest, Father Antonio Melo. Zumbi was given the name "Francisco", assisted in Catholic mass services, and was taught Portuguese and Latin. He escaped at age fifteen and returned to Palmares. In 1679, Zumbi succeeded his uncle, Ganga Zumba, and became the leader of Palmares. Zumbi is revered as the pioneer of the resistance and a hero among Afro-Brazilians today.

The Republic of New Palmares Movement begins with a change of consciousness among the people. When the Israelites were led out of Egypt and wandered in the desert for 40 years, they endured a process of exorcising the spirit of the slave in the people in order to receive the spirit of a free and independent people. After over 400 years in captivity, we have come out with "great substance". Yet, we lack the collective wisdom and "wise counsel" to convert this substance into true power. The greatest challenge we face is shifting the mind from a consumer to a producer. What are we producing as a people that others are willing to pay top dollar for its value?

The Republic of New Palmares Movement is about creating a space for African people to thrive socially, politically, economically, and culturally. It is a movement to create a space for black-owned businesses to grow and expand into multimillion and multibillion-dollar enterprises. Why am I focused on building multimillion and multibillion-dollar enterprises? Because we need businesses of size and scale to recruit our best and brightest talents graduating from college. When we put our children on a "paper chaser" journey, we run the risk of losing them to a **FORTUNE** 500 company. When that happens, we lose not only the human resources but also the financial resources. To become a real economic force, African people need to own, control and produce their financial, material, and human capital.

By only having businesses at a Mom & Pop level, African businesses have limited growth potential to become the economic empires necessary to bring about economic liberation. In **ZERO TO ONE MILLION,** Ryan P. Allis states all businesses fall under one of four categories:

1. Manufacturing
2. Distribution
3. Retail
4. Service

We tend to choose businesses and industries with little to no barriers of entry, which are easy to enter, but difficult to grow, especially service-based businesses. We tend to be heavy in retail and service, yet light to non-existent in the manufacturing and distribution sectors of business, where the money and power are most abundant. When we move into manufacturing and distribution, we can put our people to work en masse. The more we produce and distribute, the more we can evolve into a true economic force.

Part of what can make the Republic of New Palmares effective is practicing "economic synergy". What do I mean? When I come into one of our communities, I'm looking for an opportunity to do business. If I see an abundance of barbershops, hair care salons, and nail care salons, do I compete for the same dollar? Or, do I move into launching a distribution warehouse and turn my potential competitors into clients?

If I'm practicing economic synergy amongst our people, I choose to be a distributor. I create more jobs and "new money" by doing so. Now that I have clients, I need insurance on my building and equipment and health insurance for my employees. There should be a black insurance agent or a black-owned insurance company that can address my business and personal needs. That same agent or company can also ensure my clients through referrals.

Next, I need to outsource my tax, accounting, and payroll needs. I should find a black CPA or accountant who can address my needs in those areas. And, through referrals, I can recommend that CPA and/or his firm to my clients. These are examples of how New Palmares can nurture and cultivate economic synergy within its borders. We should not compete amongst ourselves, but seek to complement existing industries. By seeking to complement what already exists in the market, we can create more jobs, "new money" and strengthen the economy of the Republic of New Palmares. Create and complement your brother or sister. Do not compete with them.

The political and military aspects of New Palmares will be based on the political philosophy of Malcolm X's Black Nationalism. Each quilombo must control its political environment. The political decisions must be in the best interests of the citizens of the quilombo. The policymakers who are entrusted with the welfare of the quilombo must remember the people who put them in power, for it is the people who placed the policymaker in power and can remove him or her from power if that policymaker proves to be incompetent or treasonous.

The military aspect of the quilombo speaks to what the Honorable Elijah Muhammad taught about the three sciences a people must know and apply to building a community or nation. I added a fourth science that goes with the other three:

1. Business, Economics, and Finance
2. Diplomacy, Negotiation, and Warfare
3. Genetic Engineering/Mate Selection
4. Culture

In the science of diplomacy, negotiation, and warfare, the Republic of New Palmares must have the power to defend the political and social integrity and welfare of the quilombo. In the past, there were nearly 60 "Black Wall Streets" in America, including Rosewood (FL), Durham (NC), and Tulsa (OK). The biggest shortcoming of these enclaves was the lack of a "security force". When Tulsa was bombed from the air, it exposed the weakness of the inability to defend itself from enemy aggression.

When we begin to build the Republic of New Palmares, we must be prepared to defend its social, political, economic, and cultural welfare and integrity. The Fruit of Islam, the UNIA-ACL's African Legion, the Black Panther Party, and the New Black Panther Party are examples of the importance of the "bullet" (military) to protect the "ballot" (political), "book" (education) and "buck" (economics).

The Republic of New Palmeres does not begin with a physical location, money, businesses, or a plan. The Republic of New Palmares begins with a mission, vision, and purpose. It begins with seeing a new or different reality for ourselves. Our elder Les Brown teaches us to say "It's possible!" to our goals, dreams, and visions.

Do we believe in the possibility of building businesses of size and scale where we can employ our people and pay them a true living wage that can support themselves and their families without struggling? Do we believe in the possibility of building an economic reality of our own creation?

Can we believe in the possibility of creating culturally conscious millionaires, multimillionaires, and even billionaires who are committed to using their wealth to uplift their people and expand the prosperity and abundance we deserve?

Creating Your Five-Year Freedom Fund Plan

CREATING YOUR FIVE-YEAR FREEDOM FUND PLAN

Have you ever noticed how much energy people put into planning a vacation, wedding, or some other event? They are meticulous, paying attention to detail and ensuring that nothing is left to chance. Yet, when it comes to planning for financial freedom, that energy is non-existent. Why are people so reluctant to make plans for financial freedom? There are several reasons why people do not reach financial freedom. Some of those reasons include:

- They do not make financial freedom a priority in their lives
- They do not practice the 10% Solution
- Expenses greater than income

- Too much "bad debt" (credit card, etc.)
- No "safety net" fund
- Inadequate or nonexistent estate planning and asset protection
- Incompatible view on money with your spouse or significant other
- Lack of self-discipline
- They do not have "wise counsel" to guide them in their financial goals
- Lack of a desire to learn the Laws and Science of Money
- Lack of a strong enough "why" to become financially free
- Have not clearly defined what financial freedom means to them

Dennis Kimbro, a best-selling author of **THE WEALTH CHOICE**, says financial independence begins at $250,000 annually. Grant Cardone, the author of **THE 10X RULE**, argues that financial independence starts at $10 million. Financial freedom means different things to different people. Part of that definition must include the freedom from the "addiction" of a paycheck. If you must trade time for money to receive a check, you are not financially free.

What benefits can be experienced from achieving financial freedom? Some benefits include:

- Freedom to choose how to live your life
- Freedom from the need for a paycheck
- Creating multiple streams of income as "unemployment insurance"

- Retire early
- Pursue entrepreneurial ventures
- Have more quality time with family
- Focus on your life's work

Now the question is "How do I get there?" But more importantly, the question you need to ask yourself is "Why?". The process means nothing without a powerful Driving Force behind it. Many people are looking for that "magic bullet" to bring instant relief. Achieving financial freedom is a process that cannot be rushed. There are no shortcuts in becoming financially free. There are "freedom dues" that must be paid. There is a process of deprogramming and reprogramming your mind to be focused on wealth, prosperity, abundance, and financial freedom.

Carter G. Woodson, author of **THE MISEDUCATION OF THE NEGRO**, said it took him 30 years to undo the damage his Harvard "education" did to his mind. Many of us must undo the damage of bad information about business, economics, finance, entrepreneurship, and investing.

Five Year Financial Freedom Plan

How does one go about creating a Five-Year Financial Freedom Plan? Everything begins with a decision. That decision must become not just a goal to achieve, but a promise to yourself. That decision must only have one outcome - SUCCESS! Think of your decision to be financially independent as a new standard in your life. Tony Robbins, the author of **UNLIMITED POWER** and **MONEY**, talks of standards and rituals. In this instance, the standard has become financial independence. But what rituals do you need to embrace to reinforce the standard?

The "rituals" can serve as the action steps towards the standard. Since this is a Five-Year plan, let's convert it into months. Five years is equal to 60 months. You can go even further by breaking it down into 90-day or 12-week segments. From there, you can begin to map out the blueprint to reach the standard. Every 90 days, something should be accomplished or achieved. Every 90 days, you should be reviewing your new standard and the action steps. Every 90 days, a milestone must be reached.

What is the importance of having a Five-Year Financial Freedom Plan? A Plan gets you out of the habit of misusing and abusing money. It gives the aspiring wealth builder a blueprint and a path towards financial freedom.

When developing your Five-Year Financial Freedom Plan, here are some questions to consider:

1. **What is my "target number"?**: All wealth-builders have a "target number" that will signal financial freedom and economic independence. Dr. Dennis Kimbro states that financial freedom begins at earning $250,000 per year. Dwayne Mooney, son of legendary comedian Paul Mooney, states that financial freedom is making $5000 per month in passive income. Grant Cardone defines financial freedom as having a personal net worth of $10 million. What is your "target number"?

2. **What is your "target date" (Independence Day)?**: The wealth builder has a "target date" where s/he will be free of the need of a paycheck or working for money. "One day"

and "Someday" are not clearly defined dates.

3. **What action steps do you intend to take to reach your target number?:** The wealth builder must take a series of steps to bring him to his goal of achieving his target number to give him financial freedom and economic independence. Writing these steps on paper will allow the wealth builder to see the steps and organize them.

4. **How many streams of income/revenue will you need to reach your target number?**: The size of your target number will determine the number of streams you must create to reach your target number. It has been suggested to have four, while others say many millionaires have seven streams of income. Some of those streams must generate passive

and residual income. Warren Buffett calls it "making money in your sleep".

5. **What streams do not require your presence?**: Not every stream needs to generate earned or active income. At least one stream must be able to generate income without your presence. Affiliate marketing and other forms of e-commerce have demonstrated the power of passive and residual income.

6. **What is the mission, vision, and purpose of your business and personal financial life?:** The wealth builder must take the time to clearly define his mission, vision, and purpose for his business and personal financial life. What is the reason for pursuing wealth? Who do I aspire to be as an African-

centered millionaire? How can my wealth help African people?

RZA's Five Year Plan

RZA, a co-founder of the rap group Wu-Tang Clan, had developed a Five-Year plan to dominate the rap game. He recruited eight other emcees to travel with him on this "mission". In **THE WU-TANG MANUAL**, RZA discussed elements of his five-year plan, including:

1. Creating a deal where they sign to a label (**LOUD** Records) and allow the members to sign with other labels as solo artists
2. Use other vehicles to spread the Wu-Tang brand (clothing, comic books/graphic novels, acting, film, etc.)

When RZA developed his plan, he had to see the plan in his mind. The endgame had to be clear in his mind before it was a physical reality. There were times he would walk the streets of "Shaolin" (Staten Island), mumbling to himself about the plan and how Wu-Tang would dominate the rap game. The result of the Wu-Tang Five Year Plan included:

1. Its first two albums becoming multi-platinum classics (**ENTER THE 36 CHAMBERS** and **TRIUMPH**)
2. Launched the acting career of Method Man (**OZ, HOW HIGH** and **HOW HIGH 2, THE COBBLER, SHAFT, BELLY, POWER BOOK II: GHOST**)
3. Launched the Anime-influenced cartoon series **AFRO SAMURAI**
4. RZA as an actor (**GHOST DOG, AMERICAN GANGSTER, GANG RELATED**), director (**THE MAN WITH THE IRON FISTS**), and

executive producer (**WU-TANG: AN AMERICAN SAGA**)

5. RZA (**THE WU-TANG MANUAL, THE TAO OF WU**) and U-God (**RAW**) as best-selling authors
6. Clothing line (Wu-Wear)

Having a Five-Year Financial Freedom Plan is more of a marathon than a sprint. It requires long-term planning with achieving short-term goals and milestones along the way. Like other journeys, this one has ebbs and flows. Unfortunately, it offers no straight path. In fact, no two paths to financial freedom and economic independence are the same.

Some may choose the path of entrepreneurship and business ownership, while others choose to become investors in real estrate and companies listed on the New York Stock Exchange (NYSE) and NASDAQ. Find the path that resonates with you.

QUESTIONNAIRE ABOUT BUSINESS, ECONOMICS, AND FINANCE

1. **Age**: ______________________
2. **Occupation:**

   ____

   ____

3. **What is money to you?**

   ____

   ____

   ____

   ____

   ____

4. **What do financial freedom and economic independence mean to you?**

   ____

   ____

   ____

   ____

   ____

   ____

   ____

5. **Do you have a positive or negative about money? Why do you have this attitude?**

6. **What did your mother and/or father teach you about money?**

7. Have you considered becoming an entrepreneur? If so, have you taken steps towards making your business idea a reality? Why or why not?

8. **Do you believe African people are a "rich" or "poor" people? Why do you feel this way?**

____

____

____

____

____

9. **Would you enroll in a workshop or workshop series on business, economics and finance from an African-cantered perspective? What do you intend to learn in these workshops that can be applicable to you? What would you consider a reasonable price for a workshop or workshop series? Online or in-person? Weekday or weekend?**

____

____

____

____

10. **What does financial literacy mean to you?**

11. **Are you a "saver" or "spender"? Why?**

12. **Do you consider yourself a good and responsible steward of money? Why or why not?**

13. **How organized are your finances? What challenges do you face in organizing your finances?**

14. **What lessons do you teach children about money? Do you encourage the youth to pursue employment or entrepreneurship? Why?**

15. **How many streams of income come into your household? How many streams are beyond a job?**

16. What steps can you IMMEDIATELY take towards improving your financial intelligence, financial IQ, and personal net worth?

1.____

____

2.____

____

3.____

____

4.____

____

5.____

____

6.____

____

7.____

____

8.____

____

9.____________________________________

____

10.___________________________________

____

11.___________________________________

____

12.___________________________________

____

The purpose of this questionnaire is to give you an idea of your thoughts and attitudes are towards money, what you are doing right and where you can improve. In order to be financially free and economically independent, one must possess the mindset of financial freedom and have the economic resources to express one's financial freedom.

When I issued this survey to people, the responses I received were mind-blowing. Many still have what I consider a schizophrenic mentality towards Money. They hate it, yet prostitute themselves for it. They hate others for having an abundance of money, yet have no problem attempting to dig into their pockets for selfish means.

CULTURE, HISTORY, AND SPIRITUALITY: THE NUCLEUS OF ECONOMIC EMPOWERMENT

"Show me a people with cultural cohesiveness, and I'll show you a people who are economically prosperous."

- *Brother Minister Zumbi Y. Shawala*
  Liberty Hall Media Group

The Most Honorable Elijah Muhammad, the author of **MESSAGE TO THE BLACKMAN**, stated there were three sciences that African people need to master in order to be a free and sovereign group:

1. Business, Economics, and Finance
2. Diplomacy, Negotiation, and Warfare
3. Mate Selection and Genetic Engineering

There is a fourth science that Mr. Muhammad did not mention by name, but it played a significant role in the success of the early days of the Nation of Islam. That science is culture. What exactly is culture? According to Merriam-

Webster's Dictionary, culture is "the customs, arts, social institutions, and achievements of a particular nation, people or another social group". It further defines culture as "the attitudes and behavior characteristic of a particular social group".

Culture serves as the driving force of how people operate in the world. It impacts every aspect of human activity, including economics. Michael Imhotep, the founder of the African History Network, states that culture gives a people its "V.I.P.'s" (values, interests, and principles).

Pyramid Principle

Another aspect of culture is the Pyramid Principle. Designed by Dr. Leonard Jeffries and Professor James Smalls, the Pyramid Principle is based on three components: 1) history and culture, 2) economic power and 3) political power. At the root or base of the pyramid are history and culture. A people's activity is rooted in healthy respect and appreciation of its history and culture. Political power cannot exist without economic power.

In turn, the economic power that is not rooted in culture and history cannot serve the greatest interests of its people. When culture and history are not at the foundation of a people's activity, inappropriate decisions are made (consciously or unconsciously) that compromise the highest and greatest good of a people's social, political, economic, and cultural welfare and integrity.

Culture influences a group of people and their shared beliefs and preferences. In regards to economics, culture impacts the decision-making, management, and valuation of a people's resources.

In developing the Gospel of Afronomics Theology, I make the argument that a people's economic development and empowerment are rooted in a nucleus of culture, history, and spirituality. Culture gives a people its values and beliefs and shapes the perspective of a people's view of the world. History gives a people the ability to trace their genesis.

Spirituality gives a people its moral compass and guide its behavior inside the community and outside with other peoples. When a people's economic prosperity is firmly rooted in this nucleus, the economic decisions made will always be for the highest and greatest good of the people.

Six Axioms of Culture

In **BEYOND RACE-ISM**, the author Keidi Obi Awadu discussed his "Six Axioms of Culture". These axioms play a significant role in a people's quest for economic prosperity. There have been numerous situations where African people have accumulated millions of dollars, yet have no power in establishing and implementing policy. They lacked a culture to give them a framework of how to organize and maximize their resources to their benefit.

The six axioms are:

1. **Spirituality**: Spirituality is the cornerstone of a people's moral conduct. In other words, I am my brother's/sister's keeper.
2. **Language**: Language can serve as a barrier to protect a people's economic interests from potential competitors. Language also serves to reinforce other paradigms in a people's culture.
3. **History**: History is the acknowledgment of historical heroes and heroines. It also teaches a people to view the world through a "race first" paradigm. The Honorable Marcus Garvey

always taught to put the interests of African people first.

4. **Traditions**: Celebrations of significant holidays, birthdays of significant people within a culture, and significant events in a people's history. Examples of holidays include Kwanzaa and Juneteenth. Birthdays include Dr. Martin Luther King's Birthday (January 15), Marcus Garvey's birthday (August 17), and Malcolm X's birthday (May 19). Significant events include numerous liberation days of African nations, the release of Nelson Mandela, or record-setting events.
5. **Shared Values**: Code of Conduct (formal or informal) or principles. An example of shared values is the Nguzo Saba from Kwanzaa.
6. **Logic**: Fusion of previous axioms to create a people's thought process.

The role of culture in a people's economic prosperity cannot be overemphasized. In **GODFATHER III**, Luchessi taught Vincent Corleone that finance "is a gun. Politics is knowing when to pull the trigger." I would like to substitute "culture" in place of "politics". The role of culture in a people's economic prosperity cannot be overemphasized. It is culture that serves as the template and blueprint for a people's existence and prosperity.

A CONVERSATION WITH BROTHER MINISTER ZUMBI Y. SHAWALA

A conversation with Brother Minister Zumbi Y. Shawala, author of G.O.A.T. ***(THE GOSPEL OF AFRONOMICS THEOLOGY), the*** G.O.A.T. *book series, and what he plans to achieve and accomplish with the book series and the* ***GOSPEL OF AFRONOMICS THEOLOGY*** *movement.*

Q: Why did you choose to create the GOSPEL OF AFRONOMICS THEOLOGY book series and movement?

A: I felt African people needed a practical, functional, and empowering blueprint for economic success in the 21st century and beyond. There are plenty of concepts and theories about our economic issues and potential solutions, but rarely have I seen a blueprint designed and executed at a grassroots level. I feel the **GOSPEL OF AFRONOMICS THEOLOGY** can do what has been lacking: give African people a chance to have success with building individual and collective economic prosperity at a grassroots level.

Q: What do you intend to achieve with the GOSPEL OF AFRONOMICS THEOLOGY movement?

A: My intention is for this movement (including the book series) to catalyze African people to get to shift their consciousness about economics and how it impacts our lives. I also want to show our people how they can do something for themselves and not wait for circumstances to be favorable. To improve our financial condition as a people, we must take charge and begin to build an economic future of our creation. All we got is 'US'!

Q: What have you learned from the self-publishing experience?

A: The Bar-Kays had a saying: **Freedom is a road seldom traveled by the multitude**. This experience has been nothing short of bearing witness to the truth of that statement. For me, I learned the most important things to have are self-reliance and spirituality. When you choose to produce books as an independent author, there is a greater burden of responsibility. But with that responsibility comes a greater reward. For example, if I publish a book priced at $17.95, I receive $10.00-11.00 per book in royalties. If I am the one who bootstraps the bulk of the project and wrote the book from its idea to the completed project, then I deserve the bulk of the royalties from my work.

I also learned about the fickleness and generosity of people. Some say they are with you and support you, but only when the sun is shining. Few will stand with you during the turbulent times. The ones who do stand with you during the storms are the ones who will truly "ride or die".

For this reason, one must never do things solely for money. There must be a more profound driving force that sustains you when you embark upon a journey to produce something that is meant to transcend time and outlive its creator.

Q: Explain the concept of a "black economic liberation theology."

A: A Black Economic Liberation Theology (B.E.L.T.) is to serve as a guide to give African people a fighting chance of establishing habits and core beliefs that can serve their most significant economic and cultural best interests. This theology is a tool that African people can apply to boost and strengthen their economic lot in life. In writing this theology, I want to make things as practical and pragmatic as possible. I want to focus on the things African people **CAN** do with the resources they have.

Booker T. Washington taught us to drop our buckets where we are and build. He also stated that success leaves clues and footprints. What clues and footprints have been left for us? These clues and footprints are in the form of habits and core beliefs that have served various people's journeys to wealth, abundance, and prosperity. The habits we embrace and apply today will become the future we create for ourselves.

Q: Why should African people be concerned about economics and its role in the liberation of African people?

A: African people in America have a gross domestic product (GDP) of nearly $2 trillion inside a nation with a $19.75 trillion GDP. Yet, our productivity falls short of the target. If we have as much capital flowing through our hands, how can 44% of America's homeless be African men? Why is our unemployment rate so high, especially amongst our youth? Why is there a disproportionate number of African women with children turning to social welfare programs? We need to begin asking what we can do with the resources we have, and how we "vote with our wallets" regarding how we use or misuse our financial resources.

Q: How does economics affect the lives and livelihoods of African people?

A: Economics affects where we choose to live, where our children attend school and college, who we marry, how we will retire, how we donate to charity, and anything else that deals with our quality of life as a people. There is no way to avoid the topic of economics, so we need to understand its importance and appreciate its impact on our lives. Wu-Tang Clan was correct when it coined the phrase: **C**ash **R**ules **E**verything **A**round **M**e!

Q: What is "AFRONOMICS"?

A: I define **AFRONOMICS** as a study and application of economic principles through an African-centered or "race-first" paradigm. The issue I have with traditional economics is that it is approached from a position of scarcity and lack. As an "**Afronomicist,**" I approach economics from a position of abundance and how to create more abundance for more people through what economist Paul Zane Pilzer calls "economic alchemy." Plus, I'm looking at how our culture, history, and spirituality influence our economic decisions. **THE GOSPEL OF AFRONOMICS THEOLOGY** will be a philosophy and a movement to help African people heal our economic plight and empower our people to maximize the resources we do have. What ultimately determines our poverty or prosperity is not how we choose to apply the resources we do have and make them serve our individual and collective needs and desires, but how we think on the individual and collective conscious levels.

Q: How did you create the GOSPEL OF AFRONOMICS THEOLOGY program and philosophy?

A: I built the **GOSPEL OF AFRONOMICS THEOLOGY** from my research and personal experience of our businesses and personal financial situations. I also reached into my Africana Studies background and studied various individuals and movements, including the Honorable Marcus Garvey and his **COURSE ON AFRICAN PHILOSOPHY**, Elijah Muhammad's Economic Blueprint from **MESSAGE TO THE BLACKMAN,** as well as Baba Omowale's (Malcolm X) economic philosophy of black nationalism. I began looking at what has worked for us in the past, along with emerging trends that have made certain paths to economic prosperity obsolete. It was initially seven principles in 2006 but has grown to sixty. This process took over fourteen years of personal experience, research, and observation. This evolving journey is an example of what one can do on his or her own when driven by a mission, vision, and purpose greater than oneself.

Q: How does the GOSPEL OF AFRONOMICS THEOLOGY differ from other programs about economics and African people?

A: The **GOSPEL OF AFRONOMICS THEOLOGY** looks to meet the reader where s/he is and present a set of "tools" that can be applied daily at a grassroots level. It also seeks to explain the role of culture, history, and spirituality and their connection to a group of people's economic prosperity. Other books and programs have focused more on the issue and gave a vague, conceptual solution that requires a quantum shift of the collective consciousness of a large segment of people, which can be time and energy draining. I chose to create and focus on a pragmatic blueprint that everyone can use. It focuses on what can be done at individual, family, and community levels. The **GOSPEL OF AFRONOMICS THEOLOGY** focuses on starting with the wo/man in the mirror and expanding from there.

Q: What are the components of the GOSPEL OF AFRONOMICS THEOLOGY?

A: **The GOSPEL OF AFRONOMICS THEOLOGY** consists of sixty principles, a pyramid divided into three phases, and a "border" as displayed on my **PYRAMID OF PROSPERITY,** Phase I is "Personal Development, Power, and Growth," where you build a knowledge base and shift your consciousness. Phase II is "Creating, Building,

Earning & Expanding Wealth." This is where you are earning and investing your capital to make your wealth grow. Phase III is "Sustaining, Protecting, Maintaining and Bequeathing Wealth." This phase is where you maintain, protect and bequeath your wealth to the next generation. The pyramid is "protected" by a black border called "Culture, History & Spirituality." All economic decisions must have a cultural, historical, and spiritual foundation. I also have a Wealth Building Quadrant and a "C.H.I.C.A.G.O. Code". This is the **GOSPEL OF AFRONOMICS THEOLOGY** in a nutshell.

Q: You also have a Wealth Building Quadrant that has four stages of wealth building. Can you discuss this quadrant and how future generations of African people can apply it to their financial lives?

A: The four stages of the Wealth Building Quadrant are:

- **Phase I**: Acquisition
- **Phase II**: Earning & Investing
- **Phase III**: Sustainability, Maintenance & Protection
- **Phase IV**: Bequeathing

Each phase has an age range and what activities the individual should be doing. This square is more of a guide and not necessarily hard and fast rules. I gave an overall view of the Quadrant in Tablet #5 about the Wealth Building Quadrant. The one thing I do encourage is that future generations of African people need to become financially independent, ideally, by age 40, but no later than 50. We must break the addiction to paychecks and begin living from passive and residual income, or what I call "mailbox money." The key to becoming financially free and economically independent is to solve the riddle of how to make money in your sleep. Once you solve that riddle, you can declare your financial freedom and independence from a job. You have now liberated yourself from the addiction to a paycheck.

Q: Explain the C.H.I.C.A.G.O. Code

A: The C.H.I.C.A.G.O. Code is for every aspiring wealth builder and "Afronomicist" in how he or she must conduct himself in all business and financial affairs, especially amongst African people. There have been too many "Hotep Hustlers" and "Black

Power Pimps" that have raided and robbed the people of their financial resources. Whether it was through the promise of an institution or industry, misappropriation of funds, or outright theft, the people have been scorned by those who come with slick words and false promises, only to deceive.

The C.H.I.C.A.G.O. Code is comprised of Eight Virtues:

1. Character
2. Honor
3. Integrity
4. Courage
5. Action Oriented
6. Goal-Oriented
7. Organization

8. Ethical Excellence

Q: There has been lots of talk about the need to practice group economics. What is your perspective on group economics?

A: I'm a proponent of group economics, but the self-economics must be addressed as well. In order to have group economics, the self-economics must be sound. By addressing the individual self-economics, **THE GOSPEL OF AFRONOMICS THEOLOGY** becomes a more pragmatic blueprint for building individual wealth. As individuals build their personal wealth, they can begin to pool their resources to practice group economics. Too many times, people have preached group economics at the expense of addressing the individual self-economics, which has been problematic. People cannot give what they truly do not have to provide. The poor cannot help the poor.

Q: What role does critical thinking play in developing an economic philosophy that gives African people the opportunity to succeed?

A: Critical thinking is probably the most important component of building wealth. To transform your economic reality, you must practice critical thinking. Ben Bloom, the creator of Bloom's Taxonomy and Cognitive Domain, developed the Six Levels of Critical Thinking. These six levels can help the wealth builder to strengthen his knowledge base, understand it, apply it, analyze it, evaluate, and create it.

The Six Levels of Critical Thinking are:

1. Knowledge
2. Comprehension
3. Application
4. Analysis
5. Synthesis
6. Evaluation

The wealth builder must start with building a knowledge base that is relevant to his desire to be financially free and economically independent. He must then begin to comprehend and apply what he knows. Then, he must analyze the results he produced based on the knowledge he accumulated and organized. Next, the wealth builder makes an evaluation and an assessment to justify a decision or a course of action. Finally, the wealth builder creates by generating new ideas, products, or a different perspective on a certain situation.

Your learning must be activated by discussing it, writing about it, and applying it. In other words, imitate it, assimilate it and innovate it.

Q: Do you consider African people as a set of "poor" people?

A: No, far from it. African people have always been wealthy and rich people. We've made other races of people rich with our labor, talent, and natural resources. We've been treated like a refrigerator that never gets replenished. People constantly take from Africa and its people, but never replace or restore what was taken.

As for what we do with what we have, we make poor decisions with our resources primarily out of fear, greed, and ignorance. Dr. Martin Luther King said we've been conditioned to pay for what we want and beg for what we need. An example is the release of the Marvel blockbuster movie **BLACK PANTHER** in February 2018. Advanced ticket sales were over $200 million! And the first week's ticket sales were over $230 million domestically! Yet, we still have not solved our unemployment and underemployment issues. We must question our collective economic integrity and address our economic hypocrisy.

Now, how can we justify giving Disney over $1 billion without blinking an eye and not ask ourselves how we can be so comfortable with a youth unemployment rate of nearly 60%? Plus, we have the nerve to demand that **MARVEL** and Disney give

25% of the net profits back into the black community! WTF? Really? How about we keep that $1 billion and create our own "Hollywood"? The most effective boycott is to build your own and do for yourself.

If we look at the history of black cinema, let us study and apply the spirit of Oscar Michaeux. Let's look at Melvin Van Peebles. His independent movie, **SWEET SWEETBACK'S BADDASS SONG,** generated over $25 million in 1972. He also was the architect of guerrilla filmmaking. But I digress...

I am not against living a lifestyle of opulence and abundance. My issue is that our priorities are out of order. We have a nasty habit of creating an illusionary lifestyle **BEFORE** we build the wealth to sustain it. It is sustained wealth that affords us the lifestyle we desire.

I believe that once we empower ourselves with proper information, we will begin to take appropriate action and make more intelligent and racially responsible decisions with our resources.

Q: You say there needs to be an entrepreneurial revolution amongst African men throughout the African World community, especially America. Why are you so adamant about this revolution?

A: Because the unemployment rate is so high amongst African men, we need to look to entrepreneurship as our **FIRST** choice instead of a last resort. Also, a friend of mine once said a man could never be a true man in another man's house. If we are to be what Nature built us to be, then we must be ready, willing, and able to go and do something for ourselves. There are three things all men are created to be: producers, providers, and protectors of their respective villages.

If the brothers are going to declare themselves as men, I ask them this question: ***How can we call ourselves men if we cannot produce and provide jobs for our women?*** We seem to be the only group of men on the planet who has no issue with its women looking for employment and provision outside the race en masse.

How can a brother look himself in the face and see his wife, significant other, mother, daughter or aunt prepare herself each morning to give her labor to other races and bring home pennies in exchange for her labor? It's almost another form of pimping our women as far as I'm concerned.

I will also pose a question to the sisters: ***If another man controls the earning capacity of your man, who's really your man?*** Is it the man who signs the check, or the man who has to prostitute himself for it? You cannot declare freedom and independence when your job is dictating the economic policy of the home. Until you break the financial "chains," you will be a "paycheck junkie" and financial "prisoner" of your job.

African men must begin to shift their consciousness from "security" to "freedom" and from "consumer" to "producer." We must focus on production. It's one thing to teach a man how to fish. It's another to teach a man how to build a fishing industry that can feed his village for generations to come.

Q: Amilcar Cabral once said, a people's chances of victory in a revolution can be measured by its ability to embrace and practice a culture that is diametrically opposed to (and better than) the oppressor. How can a revolutionary entrepreneurial

culture help African people become financially free and economically independent?

A: Having a revolutionary entrepreneurial culture among African people has many benefits. One of the main benefits is gaining the confidence to produce goods and services to serve not only oneself but to a larger group. When a set of people use entrepreneurship and microenterprise as vehicles for economic empowerment, it changes the mentality of that people. They no longer think and feel like beggars who have no place in society. They feel more like contributors and producers. They add value to the lives of people through innovations in products and services and producing jobs with living wages.

It is not enough to teach a man to fish, but teach him to build a fishing industry so he can feed his village for generations to come.

Q: Why do you feel entrepreneurship is necessary for African people to improve their economic condition in America and the world?

A: History has shown that entrepreneurship and microenterprise are the most important keys to a people's economic liberation. When a people can do for themselves by producing goods and services for the marketplace, they have a lot of benefits. Economic self-reliance gives people confidence in themselves and they no longer feel like a burden to others. Economic self-reliance stimulates wealth creation amongst a people. Economic self-reliance helps a people reduce crime and improve organizations as well as discipline in their community. It also helps to strengthen and stabilize marriages. Regardless of what anyone may think of network marketing, the one thing I applaud about it is how these models encourage married couples to work together to create financial freedom and economic independence.

My main point is that if a group of people remains dependent on another set of people for their provision, they can never claim equality with the hand that feeds them. Entrepreneurship and microenterprise are part of paying "freedom dues." Baba Omowale (Malcolm X) taught us the price of freedom is death, but more than physical death. The Israelites that came out of Egypt had to "die" in the desert for a new people with a new freedom consciousness to emerge. African people must kill the slave within them.

`Q: Why do you feel there is a level of reluctance for African `people in America to go into business for themselves?

A: Entrepreneurship is not for the faint of heart. We talk about going into business and think of controlling our fate and destiny. But there are realities to owning and operating your business. You have to make payroll by Friday. You have tax issues. You have to comply with the State Department of Labor. You have to lead your staff. With great power comes great responsibility.

In an issue of the Nation of Islam's **FINAL CALL** newspaper, I learned that over 85% of African people in America who were lynched were business owners and entrepreneurs. So, anytime African people want to go and do for themselves, there is this need for white terrorism to crush any sense of black autonomy. You see this in the movie **HARLEM NIGHTS**. You also see this in the destruction of Black Wall Street by white terrorists. So, there is a historical context.

However, there is good news. The American demographic with the fastest growth of entrepreneurs is black women. Many factors impact this trend, but seeing African women pursuing commerce is a good sign. Like that song by Aretha Franklin and Annie Lennox: "Sisters are Doing It for Themselves"!

`Q: Are you saying entrepreneurship is the answer?

A: Entrepreneurship is an important piece of the puzzle to eradicate poverty. Dr. Muhammad Yunus understood that microenterprise plays a critical role in helping poor people escape poverty. Countries in

Latin America, Asia, and Africa are more inclined to utilize entrepreneurship. In America, the poor are offered a welfare system that is designed to enslave them economically.

I have no issue with preparing the poor to enter the workforce. My issue is denying people the right to pursue other options without penalty. Many black communities have been destabilized both politically and economically for well over 50 years. For African people to gain control of their fate and destiny, they need to control the economic activity in their communities. Also, those local black political officials must work to create a political climate that is conducive for African people to start and grow businesses.

Q: How should African people view entrepreneurship in the wake of COVID-19?

A: In **MESSAGE TO THE BLACKMAN**, The Most Honorable Elijah Muhammad warned there will come a day and time when the white man cannot employ his people. We've reached that point. Now we have entered a post-COVID-19 economy where people must become entrepreneurial-minded. This new economy will rely on people providing more value and solving more problems in the market.

What does that mean for African people? It means that relying on a job or single source of income is a dangerous position to be when automation and robotics have rendered your labor obsolete. Jerome Powell, chairman of the Federal Reserve Bank, stated that the pre-COVID-19 economy will never return. He further stated that the pandemic has accelerated the introduction of automation, telework, and other forms of technology.

`Q: How are money and manhood related?

A: Money and manhood go together like peanut butter and jelly, bread and butter, and burgers and fries. Men need resources to operate in life. A man with no resources is about as useful as a car with no gas in the tank. When a man has no resources to operate, he is essentially castrated. When he has to look to other men for provision and employment, he becomes a prisoner and slave to other men. Those men also dictate economic policy in their homes.

My belief is that man was built to be self-employed and entrepreneurial. Nowhere in the Torah, Bible, Quran or Bhagavad-Gita is any mention of the prophets relying on a job to sustain themselves. Each man was self-employed. My theory is that if the Universe sent the prophets to be an example for the people to emulate, then we must also look at their ability to rely on the Universe and themselves for their "daily bread."

If African people are serious about building real multigenerational wealth, then the men must think, speak and act "production" instead of "consumption." Men are built to produce, provide for and protect their "villages." African men must ask themselves every day if they are being productive. The ideal form of production is through entrepreneurship, which is ultimately the best boycott to practice.

Q: How does the prison industrial complex impact African people in America?

A: The economic cost of mass incarceration of African men in America is mind-blowing, to say the least. There are approximately 2.3 million Americans incarcerated, which is equivalent to the population of Brooklyn or Queens. One million of those incarcerated in America are black males. If these men were employed and have a weekly take-home salary of $630, we would learn that we lose over $630 million **weekly** in productivity. Nearly $1.3 billion every two weeks and nearly $32 billion annually.

Plus, we serve as the raw material for a prison industry worth over $80 billion. And we haven't discussed the domino effect this phenomenon has on how African people choose potential mates, raise children, and bring human and financial resources to the community. A community cannot survive when a significant portion of its population is in cages. Every time a brother is incarcerated, the community loses a human resource and a financial resource.

Q: What are the basic things African people can do to become more empowered about money?

A: African people can begin studying how to make money work for them instead of constantly working for money. Or, learn how to "put that dollar on the track!". African people can also learn to pay themselves **FIRST** through the 10% Solution. We need to treat ourselves with the same or greater importance as any other bill we pay religiously. We can also learn to master our emotional intelligence and develop emotional discipline, which will help us make better decisions with our resources and how to maximize them.

Q: What role does culture play in a people's economic prosperity?

A: Culture impacts a people's overall existence. Dr. Leonard Jeffries and Professor James Smalls said culture gives a people its "VIP's," meaning values, interests, and principles. There is a direct correlation between a people's cultural cohesiveness and its economic prosperity. People use culture as a protective shield to ensure its political, economic, and social welfare and integrity are kept intact. Culture instills a "race first" mentality within the group and reminds its people that they are their brother and sister's keeper.

Q: What role does politics play in a people's quest for economic empowerment?

A: Politics is simply the way people living in groups make decisions. Its purpose is to enable the members of a society to **collectively** achieve important human goals they cannot otherwise achieve individually. With those definitions, African people have to ask themselves if they have always made decisions that are in the best interests of African people.

Also, what has been the relationship between African people and American politics? Have we been able to acquire and maintain power as policymakers? More importantly, what has been our intention going into politics? Do we serve the people or serve ourselves with a check and kickbacks from those who have bought your services for their agenda to be carried out?

I sometimes feel African people do not understand that anything that is funneled through government has a political agenda. That agenda has two objectives: 1) Reward your friends, and 2) Punish your enemies. Have we been rewarded by our "friends" in the arenas of political power? History has shown that we have been punished by our "enemies" in politics via public policies that affect us politically and economically.

In a nutshell, politics is warfare. Until African people understand that politics is warfare, we will continue to be treated with benign and malignant neglect. If we are to play the "political game," we must play to win and practice "race first." Adam Clayton Powell, Jr understood that better than any other black political official we produced.

If you want to know if your elected official is acting in your best interest, remember this: who they serve is an indicator of who put them in power. Many of our political officials have been "rented" and "leased" to serve the agendas of those who write checks to fund certain political ideologies and agendas. African people are playing games with themselves thinking that getting money out of politics and pushing mass voter registration will solve the issue. White folks can't get money out of politics, so why should we think we can, especially when white folks wrote the rules of engagement? Also, there's an old saying: Politics without economics is symbolism without substance. We continue to think that voting is the be-all, end-all of all political power. Many of us have no understanding of the science of politics, much less how our elected officials have been bought off by corporations and other powerful interest groups.

Q: You talk about the psychology, language, and science of wealth creation and wealth building. Can you discuss these concepts?

A: There is psychology, language, and science to wealth creation and wealth building. Regardless of where you begin, all wealth is created from the inside. To become rich and wealthy, one must begin to think, speak and act wealthy. The first "currency" of the Universe is ideas. Everything in existence was once an idea. Dr. Dennis Kimbro states the average American gets four ideas a year. That's an average of one idea every three months. If that person chooses one idea and executes that idea with persistence, perseverance, determination, and a well-designed plan, he can achieve financial freedom and economic independence.

As for the science of wealth building, some laws govern money and how it is to be handled. Do we pay ourselves first? Do we establish financial plans (not just budgets) for our families? Do we make our money work for us? Do we protect the wealth we built? Do we know how to leverage our money? Do we understand the difference between high income and real wealth? Our money is to serve us, instead of serving money. We must **BE** rich, not just **LOOK** rich. We must create and increase value in the marketplace through our products in business and entrepreneurship.

Q: How can the GOSPEL OF AFRONOMICS THEOLOGY help African youth?

A: African youth can develop good financial habits that will serve them throughout their lives. The greatest habit is for the adults to teach (by consistent thought, word, and deed) the children to become producers as opposed to consumers. We've been trained to be consumers of other people's goods and services for too long. Our youth must apply the principles of the **GOSPEL OF AFRONOMICS THEOLOGY** and begin producing for themselves and their people. The market and the Universe are demanding producers. Consumers are like pigs: they get slaughtered because of their insatiable greed.

Q: What role does education play in a people's quest for economic empowerment?

A: Education determines how competitive we are in today's global market. I would like to discuss getting an education that is relevant and practical, especially at the collegiate level. Let's say a child attends Notre Dame, which has a tuition price of $50,000 per academic year. We're talking $250,000 for a bachelor's degree from a prestigious school. In the past, the shelf life of a college degree is four to five years. Today, the shelf life is eighteen months! Moore's Law teaches that information turns over every 18 months. A student invests five years and a quarter-million dollars into a degree where, depending on the major, the information will be rendered obsolete in less than two years. That's bad math. And, we haven't even gotten into the student loan issues.

Plus, many of the present colleges and universities are based on an Industrial Age model. There is also a prediction that 90% of all colleges and universities in America will shut down over ten years. Our students are being prepared for a world that has been out of existence for quite some time.

African people need to return to a holistic oriented model where the student is adequately prepared to handle the obstacles and challenges that will confront him. The real education begins once the student graduates from college.

Q: Do you feel the present school system in America is preparing our youth for the real world?

A: No. There is a 50-year lag time between what is taught in school and real-time. In today's world, it is not enough to know reading, writing, and arithmetic. Artificial intelligence, robotics, and automation are forcing our students and adults to stay one step ahead of technological innovation. Concerning economics, the money rules of the Industrial Age are obsolete.

When Richard Nixon took the US dollar off the gold standard in August 1971, he introduced a fiat economy into existence. Money became currency. The US dollar has lost over 97% of its purchasing power since the birth of the Federal Reserve in 1914. Now with the emergence of Bitcoin and other forms of cryptocurrency, the concept of money will take a radical shift.

Q: In your opinion, what would be considered a "quality education" in today's world?

A: A "quality education" is a lifelong journey where you are constantly pushing yourself to learn more and be more, so you can earn more. It must also improve one's humanity. If your education does not enhance or improve your humanity, morality, and ethics, then you are nothing but a beast with degrees. The two "subjects" I would teach would be personal development and financial literacy. The late Jim Rohn said if you work hard on your job, you'll make a living. But, if you work hard on yourself, you'll make a fortune. The greatest investment one can make is in himself.

In an interview, legendary motivational speaker Les Brown said he invested over $7500 in his development as a speaker through home study courses, tapes, CDs, DVDs, and attending workshops and seminars. That initial investment has led to career earnings of over $75 million. That means for every dollar he put into himself, he produced $1 million! That's one million percent return on investment. Warren Buffett can't promise a return like that, and he is considered the best as an investor. If you are searching for an investment opportunity, start with yourself.

Q: What are your thoughts on the numerous financial and business books on the market today?

A: As a collective, the financial books on the market are obsolete. They still subscribe to the Industrial Age model of economics, politics, and education. The Industrial Age of Economics ended on August 15, 1971. That date was when former president Richard Nixon took the United States dollar off the gold standard and brought America into a fiat economy. Money became currency. Instead of parking money in a bank and earning 15% in annual interest, money becomes subject to inflation.

I do not understand why these "celebrity financial gurus" continue to push money rules that are obsolete and irrelevant. The people need better and more relevant information gathered because of the radical shifts taking place in the global economy. We must treat financial literacy and economics like war. The "intelligence" gathered must be accurate and relevant to the present situation. When you attempt to fight and win a battle with obsolete and irrelevant information, you put your squadron in danger.

When the scandals of Enron, WorldCom, and Health South came in 2000-01, people should have learned that when you do not have control of your investment vehicles, you are at the mercy of those who do. That's why I would never recommend a 401(k) to people, especially after witnessing employees lose their life savings because of the wickedness of the people running those companies.

Q: Who would you recommend people read and study?

A: My recommendations concerning business, economics, and finance are Grant Cardone (**www.grantcardone.com**), Garrett Gunderson (**www.wealthfactory.com**), Sherry Peel Jackson

(**www.SherryPeelJackson.com**), Robert Kiyosaki (**www.richdad.com**), Loral Langemeier (**www.lorallangemeier.com**), and Sharon Lechter (**www.sharonlechter.com**). Their books, courses, and services are in line with what the present economic trends are and how people can create their economy, financial freedom, and economic independence. From a cultural standpoint, I recommend Mwalimu Baruti's **ASAFO** and **IWA**, the Honorable Marcus Garvey's **COURSE OF AFRICAN PHILOSOPHY**, the Honorable Elijah Muhammad's **MESSAGE TO THE BLACKMAN**,

Dr. Amos Wilson's **BLUEPRINT FOR BLACK POWER**, Dr. John Henrik Clarke's **NOTES FOR AN AFRICAN WORLD REVOLUTION** and Dr. Na'im Akbar's **NEW VISIONS FOR BLACK MEN**.

Q: There seems to be a sense of urgency amongst mainstream black leadership to address the income and wealth gap between whites and melanoid peoples in America. What are your thoughts about this issue?

A: Part of the problem is that we feel we must keep up with white people. Why would I want to compare myself to a people whose nation (America) has a trillion-dollar deficit and is the #1 debtor nation on Earth? Who said whites are the example to follow?

In Dr. Na'im Akbar's **NEW VISIONS FOR BLACK MEN**, he states that men define themselves and create their own realities through building industries and institutions. As a people, are we about the business of creating a standard of ethical economic excellence that is pleasing and acceptable to ourselves? If we are, then we have no time to "keep up with the Joneses". We have to be about the business of defining reality for ourselves and stop playing "catch up" to white people.

Q: What can economic public policy do to help black businesses gain access to capital, especially venture capital and angel investors?

A: When building an economic community, and economic policy must be developed and enforced. What is a policy? A policy is a principle to guide decisions and achieve rational outcomes. Policies have a cycle that has several steps. One of the more popular policy cycles has five steps:

1. Agenda Setting/Problem Identification
2. Policy Formulation
3. Decision Making
4. Implementation
5. Evaluation

Now, let's say we want to create a public economic policy for African people. We realize that to help African people achieve economic self-sufficiency, they must first identify a specific issue that demands attention from the public and private sectors. Let's say the issue is the need for access to equity funding for black entrepreneurs to start and grow businesses. The issue is presented to the local Black Chamber of Commerce and City Council about creating an equity fund earmarked for starting and growing black businesses (policy formulation).

After a series of meetings, public forums, research, and proposals, a decision is made. The funding will come from a combination of sources:

1. Public/Non-Profit Sector
2. Black Business Sector
3. Corporate Sector
4. Individual Contributors

The implementation of this fundraising project can last over three years, with an estimated goal of $60 million. The funds will be deposited at a designated financial institution and have the account managed by an elected team of money managers.

Over the three years, deposits are made by certified check, money order, or direct deposit.

After three years, the policy can be evaluated for its effectiveness in the intent and results. There must also be an examination of the impact and outcome of the economic public policy.

If African people can begin to formulate and enforce economic policies that are in their best interests, they can begin to put their resources to work for them. African people can begin to recycle their money and use it to build a community of, by, and for themselves.

Q: There's a resurgence of the discussion of reparations for African people in America. There is also a movement called the American Descendants of Slavery, which is focused on reparations for African descendants of the enslaved Africans in

America. What is your position on reparations from an economic perspective?

A: From what I have seen, I don't know if people truly understand what reparations are. The word "reparation" is a noun form of the verb "to repair". Money is only a minute part of the reparations experience. Also, the reparations issue cannot be addressed within the confines of the United States.

Malcolm was correct in his analysis of bringing the United States before the United Nations and the World Court on charges of genocide and crimes against humanity. From my perspective, I don't see the (Black) American Descendants of Slavery seeking to make this a global issue. Are they allowing other entities off the hook?

As far as economics is concerned, history has shown that entrepreneurship and microenterprise have been critical factors in lifting oppressed people out of poverty. The issue has been accessing capital for aspiring black entrepreneurs to launch and expand their enterprises. Also, racism and white hegemony have created barriers for black entrepreneurs to compete in the marketplace via monopolies.

If I were asked to develop an economic proposal for reparations, I would look at what was promised to African people coming out of slavery. Each was promised 40 acres, two mules, and $100 to start, along with food and medical care. In doing the math, there are nearly 60 million Africans in America. As a collective, from 1865 to today, African people are owed over $4.3 trillion in today's money. If I had to take an educated guess, each African person is owed approximately $20-30 million.

Next, I would develop a program to help black entrepreneurs become competitive in the global and domestic markets. In the US, many black businesses generate less than $10 million in annual revenue. Plus, many are in the retail and service industries, as opposed to the manufacturing and distribution sectors of business.

Q: What role can the Universal Basic Income have when discussing reparations for African people?

A: The UBI can be a catalyst used to lift African people out of an impoverished condition. With the rapid rise of artificial intelligence, automation, and robotics, over two-thirds of American jobs will disappear over the next 10 years. What does that mean for African people? In Jeremy Rifkin's **THE END OF WORK**, it talks about how African people have been the victims of technological advancement. The UBI can help African people stabilize households, increase savings, and have seed money to start businesses.

Q: With over $2 trillion in purchasing power, why do African people continue to operate in poverty and bankruptcy?

A: We have not realized what **TRUE** wealth is. Dr. Dennis Kimbro states that all wealth begins in the mind and ends in the purse or wallet. If we continue to see ourselves as "poor" people, we will never realize the tremendous wealth we possess at our fingertips. African people have been blessed with a continent that is rich in natural resources and empowers the economies of other nations.

We've been blessed with creativity and innovation that continues to set trends and transform the world to this day. African people must realize that wealth, abundance, and prosperity are rooted within us, not in what we may or may not possess. Wealth is in the mind and heart, and we must bring that wealth and share it with ourselves and the world.

Q: Would you say that Post Traumatic Slave Disorder has been (and continues to be) a critical factor in why we have not progressed economically?

A: Without question. When I look at the behavior of African people in regards to economics, I realize we are not in our right frame of mind. Our ancestral teacher, Dr. Amos Wilson, stated that the pathological and dysfunctional behavior of African people is a political and economic necessity for

America to operate and thrive. America's wealth, abundance, and prosperity have always been at our expense.

Our ancestral psychiatrist, Dr. Patricia Newton says a disorder is a disruption. We were rudely disrupted and interrupted to the point where we find ourselves in our present condition. When we continue to find ourselves as spectators at the feast, begging for crumbs from the Emperor's Table, we continue to be treated like stray dogs with no place to go.

Q: You say that welfare is "an insidious form of slavery." How is welfare a form of slavery?

A: In Randy Gage's **WHY YOU'RE BROKE, DUMB AND STUPID**, he states that the biggest threat to a government is the individual who is wealthy and independent of government provisions. The perfect citizen is the one who is dependent on the government because the more he relies on the government, the more control that government has over him. In the case of welfare, the more a person relies on it, the more control that system has over the participant.

Ideally, the welfare system should serve as a "bridge" to help an individual or family get back on its feet during a difficult time. In other words, welfare should be a "hand up" instead of a "handout." What has happened is that the welfare system cripples the individual's ability to be self-reliant. It punishes anyone determined to be self-reliant and rewards those who choose to remain attached to the system.

It becomes an insidious form of slavery because it is designed to make you dependent on it for provision. It begins to control your earning capacity and twists the minds of those who are in the system. They have been tricked into thinking the better option is to remain a slave than to work towards their freedom from that system.

Having gone through the welfare system myself, I never wanted anyone to control my fate and destiny. I want to determine my earning capacity and how I earn it. I want to determine what I can purchase from a grocery store. As a vegetarian, I want to choose food that fits my nutritional pattern and lifestyle. When a system begins to gain control over what you eat, how you eat, and when you receive an allotment to purchase groceries, you have become a slave to the system.

Q: What role does land play in a people's quest for economic prosperity?

A: Land is the basis of all political and economic power. The land is what gives a people its food supply and mineral wealth. However, a land without the knowledge to maximize its wealth is useless. Africa is the richest continent on Earth. Yet, the indigenous people of the continent are unable to extract the wealth from the earth and use it for their benefit. Centuries of colonial rule by foreign invaders have made Africa a refrigerator that continues to be raided with no intention to replenish it.

The verdict on China is "guilty" of becoming the latest colonizer of Africa. Former South African president Thabo Mbeki was right in questioning China's intentions on African soil, especially with China seeking to permanently relocate nearly 300 million Chinese citizens to Africa over the next decade and they are all men! We are beginning to see Chinese men marry local women in countries like Uganda and creating an Afro-Chinese population that will play a critical role in Africa's fate and destiny. Plus, with China pouring billions of dollars into Africa's infrastructure, who will reap the benefits of this "alliance"?

In **MESSAGE TO THE BLACKMAN**, The Honorable Elijah Muhammad stated that African people would need over 100 million acres of land (approximate size of California) to feed, clothe and shelter nearly 60 million African people in America. He also instructed us to get some of this good earth to call our own. Now is the time to heed those instructions.

Q: You've coined the terms "Afrofuturology" and "Afrofuturist." Could you explain these terms and their relevance to economic empowerment for African people?

A: I posed the question: ***Why do we have more black historians than black futurists***? This is no disrespect to the Black Studies Movement or any of its practitioners who teach it. But there must be a cadre of African people who can study present trends and make forecasts of what is to come. Who will be our version of Alvin Toffler? Who will write the black version of **MEGATRENDS**? In defining "Afrofuturology," I define it as the "science or study that deals with the future predictions and possibilities based on current trends viewed through an African-centered paradigm."

Q: How can one become an "Afrofuturist"? Is there a curriculum or program that one can take?

A: Anyone can declare himself an Afrofuturist. Through the power of "kujichagulia" (self-determination) and rigorous study, one can become an Afrofuturist. For me, the best example of an "Afrofuturist" would be Dr. Amos Wilson. His proficiency in areas of political science, economics, psychology, and sociology have made him one of our brightest scholarly minds. He also applied the knowledge of these disciplines to solving the issues of African people. The three main paths to becoming an Afrofuturist are:

1. Develop an ability to forecast the future with empirical evidence
2. Be able to envision the future through writing and intuition
3. Be prepared to create the future through

planning and consulting

The most critical component of becoming an Afrofuturist is to start with quality information from reputable sources (Credibility is a delicate asset). Also, watch for the merging of different disciplines. Afrofuturists can come from any discipline but must be prepared to study other disciplines. Finally, an Afrofuturist must be ready to invent the future. In the case of economic empowerment, the Afrofuturist must ask and answer these questions:

1. What kind of (economic) future do I envision for African people?
2. What will it take to bring that economic future into reality?
3. What challenges confront us to bring this economic future into fruition?

4. Who do we have to become to create a better economic future and a brighter economic reality for African people?

Q: Who are the "advisors to the king (or queen)"?

A: I have designated ten positions in the entrepreneur or wealth builder's "cabinet" to serve as a nucleus of "wise counsel" at his discretion in his wealth-building journey. Business, investing and wealth-building is a team effort. No one ever reached financial freedom and economic independence as a lone wolf. That's why the story of the "self-made millionaire" is a myth at best. The eight positions in the wealth builder's cabinet are:

1. Accountant/CPA
2. Attorney/Lawyer
3. Asset Protection Attorney

4. Estate Planning Attorney
5. Tax Attorney
6. Banker
7. Business Advisor/Mentor/Coach
8. Certified Financial Planner
9. Insurance Agent/Broker
10. Real Estate Agent/Broker

There will be more positions added to your cabinet as your wealth expands and grows. It is good to build it **BEFORE** the big money arrives. You don't want to have money flowing and no infrastructure or wise counsel to guide you as to maximize the best usage of your profits.

Q: Can you explain what an "Entrepreneurial Bushido" is?

A: Every successful entrepreneur possesses eight skill sets:

1. Sales
2. Marketing
3. Product Development
4. Raising Capital
5. Copywriting
6. Networking
7. Negotiation
8. Cashflow Management

For startup entrepreneurs, over 80% of their time and energy must be invested in sales, marketing, product development, copywriting, and raising capital. The mistake many startup entrepreneurs make is focusing on activities that do not bring in revenue. Nothing happens unless and until a sale is made. Jim Koch, CEO, and Founder of Boston Beer Company learned a valuable lesson from his uncle about sales. He said if sales aren't made, the company won't survive. In the beginning stages of any business, sales are paramount to the company's bottom line. You have to "make it rain in the club" to survive in business. Nothing happens unless and until a sale is made.

Q: What do you mean by "Get Your Biz Legit"?

A: Too many of us who claim to have businesses have nothing but hobbies masquerading as businesses. To be taken seriously, you must get your business and financial house in order. That means separating your personal assets from your business assets. I can show people a ten-step process of how to legitimize their business for less than $1000. The most significant expense will be filing your Articles of Incorporation or Articles of Organization for a limited liability company (LLC).

I do not recommend a DBA Sole Proprietorship or Partnership. The business world will not take you seriously nor recognize you as a legitimate business. Plus, you cannot protect your assets from a potential lawsuit. You need a complete separation and establish a separate entity (or entities) to do business. In most cases, the entity of choice for most startup businesses is either an LLC or Subchapter S corporation.

Now I'm only speaking as a layman. I highly recommend that you find an accountant or attorney who can guide you in choosing the best entity (or entities) for your business and financial situation. If you are serious about building wealth, you must get your biz legit so you won't be caught "riding dirty".

Q: What is the "nucleus" of a people's economic prosperity?

A: The "nucleus" consists of culture, history, and spirituality. This is the foundation of a people's economic success. Culture gives a group of people the framework to view themselves and how they interact with the world. History teaches people who they are, what they have accomplished, and how they came to be. Spirituality gives a people its moral and ethical compass. I define spirituality based on four components:

1. Self-Knowledge
2. Self-Awareness
3. Self-Discovery
4. Self-Mastery

In order for African people to become economically successful, this nucleus must be at the center. When this "nucleus" is firmly established, our decisions will be more appropriate and serve the best economic interests of African people. To demonstrate the importance of a strong nucleus, look at the Japanese and European Jews.

The Japanese suffered two atomic bombs, which brought World War II to an end. From 1945, the Japanese worked to build a new society. By the 1980s, Japan became a global economic force in the market. I can remember when people took Japanese as part of their business curriculum in college. European Jews lost six million in the concentration camps of Poland and Germany. The one thing that Adolf Hitler did not destroy was the cultural cohesiveness and self-identity of European Jews. They drew on their culture, history, and spirituality to overcome their tragedy.

Q: What is "culturally conscious capitalism"?

A: To me, culturally conscious capitalism is a mindset of how capitalism and business can benefit the African Diaspora. Many in the culturally conscious community would argue that capitalism is the problem. In my opinion, it is the heart of man that is the issue. If the heart is morally corrupt and spiritually bankrupt, then corruption and bankruptcy will play themselves out in any and every political and economic system.

The Europeans have betrayed every political and economic system we embraced. Even capitalism. America is not a purely capitalistic nation. If it were, why is there a police force? Public transportation? Fire department? These would be considered elements of socialism.

African people must understand that the nucleus of a people's economic prosperity is its culture, history, and spirituality. This nucleus influences every financial decision made on an individual and collective level. The resources of African people should work for their highest and greatest good.

Being a culturally conscious capitalist means a cause greater than profit drives the entrepreneur and wealth builder. An example of that cause is a clearly defined social mission. That mission serves as a guide to ensure the company remains in alignment with its core beliefs and values.

Cultural consciousness and capitalism do not have to be mutually exclusive. The mind and heart of the practitioner guide the system, not the other way around. Whatever political or economic system African people choose; it must be tailored to meet the needs of the people. We have always "Africanized" any political, economic, or religious system to fit our unique situations.

Q: What are your thoughts concerning black athletes and entertainers making financial contributions to black causes?

A: I may be in the minority with my position, but I stand behind it. I feel there's a tendency for us as a people to look to athletes and entertainers for leadership and finance, which is a huge mistake. Our gladiators and court jesters should not be placed in a position for which they are not trained.

Many will say that athletes and entertainers should do things for African people. I used to be of that school of thought. Now, I take the position of looking to the Universe and the Ancestors to support me in my endeavors. I've learned that man is too fickle for me to have that kind of faith or belief. Man cannot be **THE** Source, but he can be a way to deliver the resources. I refuse to place myself at the mercy of the fickleness or generosity of another man, especially when it comes to the economic liberation of African people.

Also, I find it hypocritical for certain elements of the culturally conscious community to refer to our professional athletes and entertainers as "slaves." Yet, they beg these same "slaves" for some of their "slave money." You can't have it both ways. If you label them as "slaves," then you can't ask them for their "slave resources."

I believe we need our athletes and entertainers, but we must offer them something in return. We cannot approach them with a hat in hand, begging and groveling for money. Offer them a business card and speak to them about our products and services that can help them. Offer them information that can enhance their cultural awareness. We must let them know that they are not alone. We support them not only as great athletes but also support them as brothers and sisters.

Q: In conclusion, what do you see for African people concerning economic empowerment?

A: I see African people at a crossroads. It is the best and worst of times. Some will view our condition as a crisis, while others see an opportunity. I'm not concerned as much about our survival as I am about our desire to live. We have proven we can survive. The question is whether we can live.

As we improve our economic condition, can we begin to build generational wealth to break the generational "curse" of poverty? Can we move to become producers and not relying on others for employment? The time has come for African people to own and control the resources we have and be the primary beneficiaries of our labor.

Q: Thank You, Brother Minister, for sharing your thoughts with the people.

A: Thank you for the opportunity to express them. I hope this dialogue can stimulate thought and lead to taking appropriate action to resolve the economic issues confronting our people across the globe.

An Economic Letter to the Unborn African

Dear Future Unborn African:

May this letter be received in the best of holistic health and spirits.

By the time you read this, I will either be an elder or an ancestor. As I write this letter to you, I write it with mixed feelings. I'm writing this to you as an apology for the failure of my generation to prepare you (economically) with the proper tools and information to navigate the world you face now. We did not provide wise counsel to you. We did not provide the necessary resources for you to build a reality of your own. For those failures, I am truly sorry.

I am also writing from a place of hope and assurance. I know that you are the future of African people. You are becoming more entrepreneurial and more business savvy than previous generations. You are beginning to answer the million-dollar question I pose to African people: Do you want liberation and your own situation…or better treatment on the plantation? You must be clear on the direction you choose. There can be no confusion in combat.

If you choose the path of liberation, you must realize that self-reliance and spirituality are your greatest "weapons" in your fight for economic freedom. You cannot demand equality when you rely on another group of people to feed, clothe, and shelter yourself. When you are at the mercy of another man's generosity for food, clothing, shelter, protection, employment, education, and medical care, you are not free.

You cannot demand equality through boycotts, which are tantamount to temper tantrums. That is just an emotional reaction and not a well-thought strategy to achieve an objective. Like chess, you must have a well-established beginning, midgame, and endgame to your economic freedom.

The most important thing for you is to have cultural, historical, and spiritual congruency and integrity. You cannot preach liberation and practice plantation politics. There have been too many Sambos amongst our people who have proven to be enemies of the African World Community. Why has this "Judas Factor" become such a threat to our aspirations for economic liberation?

There were those of us who were afraid to lose the crumbs they've received from Caesar's table and would never take the chance to build our own bakeries and bake our own bread. They were hell-bent on sabotaging liberation because it posed a threat to their addiction to those "butter biscuits" from Massa for their betrayal and treachery.

There were also cadres of "Hotep Hustlers" and "Black Power Pimps" that dwelled among us. And they will slither their way into your ranks. They will come with the greeting words of peace and blessings, be it "As-Salaam Alaikum", "Hotep", "Free the land!" or "on a MOVE!". Then, they will create elaborate schemes and scams to rob and exploit the people of their financial resources for personal gain at the expense of the people.

These cults of personality come with pretty words and sharp oratorical skills. Once they gained the confidence of the people, they bring a con game to fleece the money from the people. Some of these Hotep Hustlers and Black Power Pimps have taken thousands of dollars from the people with little to no accountability. These parasites must be identified, addressed, and brought before the people to give an account.

If they promised a school, ask for transparency of the financial records. If they ask for seed capital, ask for a proposal of the breakdown of how the money will be used. As an "investor", you have the right to know how the money is used.

I don't know what your world will become over the next 2-3 generations. I do know that what I am bequeathing to you will give you the core beliefs and principles needed to be a good steward of your resources and a responsible handler of the power you possess. I hope that you will take the baton from your elders and ancestors and run with authority, confidence and compassion.

Run with the authority that nothing, including white hegemony, will stop you. Run with confidence, knowing that the ancestors stand with you as you move into the future. Run with compassion for those who have been broken from the stress and brutality of a system that has oppressed, suppressed, repressed, and depressed them.

I know that we will survive. But I don't want you just to survive. I want you to thrive and prosper. I want you to be free. I want you never to have to ask another race for food, clothing, shelter, employment, education, protection, and medical care. I desire to help you succeed where I have failed. This book series is my gift to you. I write this as if someone were to present this book series to me as a youth.

In warfare, one must have resources to fight and win. One of the issues I had was that our people were not financially equipped to finance their war for economic liberation. It was one of the most perplexing and confusing aspects of our economic liberation movement. That is why I encourage your generation to "be forever free." Jobs as you once knew them are outdated. You must become even more entrepreneurial and sovereign.

I am forecasting that by the time you read this book, America is becoming (or already has become) a predominantly self-employed nation. You will also deal with a world that is more decentralized but will also present greater opportunities to create your own niche. I call this era the "New Age Chitlin' Circuit." It will be an era where there is great upheaval over the destruction of the old paradigm and a new one emerging with infinite possibilities. My desire is for this book series to prepare you for the opportunities to come

It will be the worst of times for some and the best of times for others. As I write this letter to you, I am witnessing a reality reconstruction causing great upheaval, turmoil, and uncertainty. However, I see a world where African people will be restored to their rightful place in human history.

I envision African people emerging from the shackles and chains of racism, poverty, low self-esteem, and regaining a true knowledge of oneself. We have survived a holocaust more brutal and vicious than the one in Europe. Yet, we still found a way to be humane, kind, peaceful, and gentle. Dr. John Henrik Clarke said we gave the world its first humanity. After over 500 years of oppression, fate may be preparing us to provide the world its next humanity.

The one warning I must give you is not to become "ethnic cheerleaders" and not heed the lessons of your predecessors. It is one thing to celebrate the accomplishments of the Honorable Marcus Garvey, Madame CJ Walker, and A.G. Gaston. It's another to take those lessons and put them to work in your era. We've had enough cheerleading. Now we must put these core beliefs and principles of G.O.A.T. into practice. When you read this book series, I don't want accolades. If you truly want to honor me, put my philosophy to work for the economic betterment of African people.

Always remember the importance of economics in building a community. More importantly, remember that economics sits on the nucleus of culture, history, and spirituality. Be good stewards of the resources (especially human resources) given to you by the Universe and ancestors.

Sincerely,

Brother Minister Zumbi Y. Shawala

S.O.A.P. (Servant of African People)

An Economic Message To The African Man

Dear African Man:

May this letter be received in the best of health and spirits.

As I write this letter to you, I want to talk about the importance of preparing your family to have multi-generational wealth. Too many of us do not take the time to protect the financial welfare and integrity of our families. When we transition and return to the essence, what do we leave our families?

There's a cautionary tale I tell young men and young activists about the financial protection of one's families when serving the people. As much as I love Malcolm and aspire to live with a similar moral code, he made the mistake of leaving the financial welfare and integrity of his family at the mercy of another man's generosity.

Malcolm believed that should anything happen to him, the Nation of Islam would take care of Sister Betty and the children. When the split occurred between Malcolm and the Nation, he was taken to court by the NOI for eviction.

Plus, he was frantically working on his memoir with Alex Haley to be published because he lamented of his failure as a provider for his family. He even attempted to take out a life insurance policy on himself, but no insurance company would insure him because they considered him too big of a risk. He wanted to get the book out so that the family could receive royalties from the book.

Although Malcolm never lived to see the final draft of his book, his wish of Sister Betty receiving royalties was fulfilled by Grover Press.

Now, what if Sister Betty had not received royalties? How would she be able to raise six daughters on her own? In fact, it took Harlem gangster legend Ellsworth "Bumpy" Johnson to cover the expenses of Malcolm's funeral. So, as much as we say we loved Malcolm, Bumpy took it upon himself to ensure one of Harlem's Finest had a proper burial.

My main point is that if we are to truly be men, we must provide for our families so that they want for nothing. We can no longer afford to be selfish and not provide the multi-generational wealth necessary to sustain the financial welfare and integrity of our families.

I recommend that every brother go watch the interview with Damon Dash on **THE BREAKFAST CLUB**. Regardless of what you thought of his delivery, Dash was on point when he spoke about building something to bequeath to one's children. We cannot bequeath a job, credit cards, welfare, or a "hustle" to our children. We must stop making our babies begin at ground zero every 20-30 years while their counterparts have a head start of tangible and non-tangible resources.

What are we teaching our children about how to be good stewards of money, land, labor, information, and the ability to organize these resources to work in their favor? Until we change our perspective about preparing our families to be financially well off, we will do our families a disservice and place them at the mercy of other people's generosity.

One of the first things we as men must do is begin building an estate. An estate can begin with the purchase of life insurance. We must also learn about the use of corporations and trusts to ensure the wealth we build now will be in the hands of our families for years to come.

As we acquire and bequeath tangible resources, we must also acquire and bequeath the intangible resources to maintain and protect the wealth. A popular saying is that the first generation earns it, the second generation spends it and by the third generation, the wealth is gone. We must protect ourselves from the squandering of the resources we do have.

The Universe and the Ancestors did not place us on this Earth to be servants to other people. God never commanded Adam to have dominion over other men. You will never find it in the Torah, Bible, or Quran. You were put here to be sovereign and autonomous. You weren't brought into existence to serve white hegemony. You were here to create a new reality for African people. You were here to build and leave a legacy and to make the world better when you leave than when you entered.

I implore you, black man. Go and do for yourself. The Prophet Muhammad (PBUH) said a man should collect twigs, bundle them and sell them as firewood than beg in the streets for provision. Go collect your twigs.

Your Brother,

Brother Minister

Zumbi Y. Shawala, S.O.A.P.

(Servant of African People)

"It's not how much money you make, but how much money you keep, how hard it works for you, and how many generations you keep it for."

- Robert Kiyosaki

An Economic Message To The African World Community

An Economic Message To The African World Community

Dear African World Community:

May this letter be received in the best of health and spirits.

As I was writing this book, I thought about how this book will help our people in different parts of the African World Community. I was expressing my apologies to a South African brother who was one of the first to read the working draft manuscript. I apologized to him because I felt I didn't include the rest of the African World Community. I was writing from an American perspective. He told me there was no need to apologize because he felt those same principles can help our people on African soil. I received the same sentiment from a South African psychologist.

I went back into the teachings of the Honorable Marcus Garvey, Booker T. Washington, and Baba Omowale (Malcolm X) to understand how we can begin to obtain and preserve our financial freedom and economic independence. They all understood when you produce goods and services, you begin to create employment opportunities for the people in the community. It eliminates the need to boycott and picket someone else because they won't hire us. Instead of begging for crumbs and scraps from another man's table, we need to be about the business of building our own bakeries and baking our own bread.

I want to know how this book series can help the Diaspora achieve economic liberation. One thing I do know is that we need to be producers and have an entrepreneurial revolution amongst ourselves. Throughout history, oppressed people have used entrepreneurship as a means to lift themselves from the shackles and chains of poverty. If we choose to take care of each other, we can radically reduce our unemployment rate by at least 75%.

Also, we need to learn to use our culture as a weapon to break the chains of poverty. The susu concept has been beneficial to raise capital to launch our ventures. We were crowdfunding long before a KickStarter or IndieGoGo . We knew the power of collective saving. The National Bureau of Economic Research did a study and learned that saving in a group triples your chances of saving. The biggest challenge is trust. I have a saying that a people who can maintain cultural cohesiveness can achieve economic prosperity. Culture is part of a three-part formula to achieve economic prosperity.

We must also reassess what education will mean to us in the 21st century and beyond. Our ancestral scholar Dr. Amos Wilson taught that the sole purpose of why European people chose to "educate" African people is to train us to serve them and solve their problems. As a people, we must ask ourselves what kind of human being is necessary to build a world of, by, and for African people. Many of us have placed our children into independent African-centered schools, only to have them working for non-African entities in the private, non-profit, and government sectors. What good is having a true knowledge of self when you still rely upon your enemy for provision? Dr. John Henrik Clarke taught that powerful people will never teach powerless people to the point where they become a threat.

The Honorable Elijah Muhammad taught there were three sciences our people need to know and master to build communities and nations:

1. Business and Economics
2. Diplomacy, Negotiation, and Warfare
3. Genetic Engineering/Mate Selection

I will add a fourth science we must master: the science of culture. If culture is not at the root of our economic liberation movement, the other sciences become useless and irrelevant. Culture not only influences the identity of a people but also its decisions in areas of economics, education, entertainment, labor, law, politics, religion, sex, and war. As a people, our behaviors in these areas of human activity must be driven and influenced by our culture.

As a son of Africa, I want to make my contribution to the economic liberation of the African Diaspora. I want us to break free of the shackles and chains put on us by entities such as the IMF and World Bank. Debt has been one of the most insidious forms of enslaving our people. We've experienced sharecropping on a global level. Now, we must break those chains and funnel those resources into the Diaspora to strengthen our various infrastructures and begin to build industries and jobs for our people.

As a student of the Honorable Marcus Garvey, I have revisited his Course of African Philosophy and his Philosophies and Opinions. His vision of African industrialization is very relevant today. The only thing he lacked was a sound infrastructure and competent people in critical positions. This book series seeks to address how infrastructures can be built and maintained to handle economic growth.

As one who studied the economic blueprint of the Honorable Elijah Muhammad, I learned the importance of acquiring land to produce the goods we consume. The Messenger taught us how to crowdfund long before KickStarter, IndieGoGo, or GoFundMe. He, along with Mr. Garvey, taught us not only to "Buy Black", but also "Build Black". Our long-term goal must be to become the #1 employer of our people.

There is a global economic "perfect storm "ahead, and we must be prepared for the "Age of Turbulence". The days of economic colonization are coming to an end. Now is the time for us as a collective, to prepare for the day when we are in the driver's seat and doing for ourselves. The victory is ours. All we need to do is open a can of whoop-ass to claim what is rightfully ours.

Sincerely,

Brother Minister Zumbi Y. Shawala, S.O.A.P.

(Servant of African People)

An Economic Message to the Potential White Ally

Dear Potential White Ally:

May this letter be received in the best of health and spirits.

As a man of African origin, I can bear witness to the vicious and venomous nature of global white insecurity (so-called white supremacy). This system has used every weapon available to demonize, vilify and criminalize me, my people, and my culture. Yet, after over 500 years of systematic and institutional gangsterism and terrorism, African people still stand before the world, fighting the good fight to restore our dignity and humanity as a people.

I've noticed a cadre of whites who want to serve as potential allies of melanoid peoples to eradicate the system of global white insecurity and restore it with a system of peace, love, harmony, unity, respect, and justice. The acknowledgment of the existence of an economic problem and the desire to be a part of the solution is always the first step. However, many of you feel helpless as to what you can do to assist us in our quest to achieve economic justice and restore order.

I would begin by understanding that racism is a system that I define in a formula:

$R = FP^2$

R = Racism

F = Fear

P^2 = Prejudice x Power

Racism is a by-product of the need for European domination over dark-skinned people. It has no real logic because it is driven by fear. According to Dr. Frances Cress Welsing, the racist or white hegemonic is driven by a deep-rooted fear of white genetic annihilation. In other words, the Fear of a Black Planet.

Begin listening and reading the stories of melanoid people. An African proverb teaches that until lions have historians, the hunter will always be the hero. The propaganda that has been fed to both of us has created a false sense of white hegemony and black inferiority. Knowing the truth of what black, brown, red, and yellow people have contributed to the advancement of civilization helps to rid your mind of how you have been conditioned to view dark-skinned peoples.

What you have been fed is nothing but propaganda. You are fed this daily diet of disinformation and misinformation to criminalize, demonize, vilify and dehumanize melanoid peoples to justify their extermination and perpetuate the agenda of white hegemony and white elitism. As you dwell amongst melanoid peoples for yourself, you begin to realize the lies you've been fed. You realize your leadership cannot be trusted. You begin to realize the wool that has been pulled over your eyes. As Brother Malcolm said "You've been had! You've been taken! Hoodwinked! Led astray! Run amuck!"

As potential allies, you must realize that melanoid peoples are coming to reclaim that which was taken. Since my birth in August 1970, I've come to learn that this world is built on one premise - **POWER**! For economic justice to be restored, melanoid peoples must have the financial freedom and economic independence to define their own reality. There are questions you must ask yourselves when you choose the position of the white ally:

1. Do I suffer from the "Fear of a Black Planet Syndrome"? Globally, whites make up less than 4% of the global population. Now, the death rate of whites has surpassed its birth rate. Fertility banks and marriage incentives have exploded in European countries.

2. Am I prepared to operate in a world seeing dark-skinned faces in positions of authority and power? Your children and grandchildren are already accustomed to this new reality.

3. Am I willing to commit "treason" and stand up to the economic machinations of global white insecurity?

4. Am I willing to assist melanoid people in transferring wealth, power, and resources back into the hands of the rightful stewards?

5. What sacrifices am I willing to make in replacing racism/white insecurity with a system of Universal Justice? This is a quid pro quo universe, and you must realize that peace, love, and economic justice come with a price tag. That price may come in the form of risking one's white skin privilege and/or one's white life.

6. What kind of world do I desire for my posterity? Your children are already accustomed to seeing dark-skinned faces in positions of power and authority.
7. What can I do as a potential white ally to bring reparations to African people on a personal and collective level and push the envelope for legislation on restorative economic justice?

Now, let me give some solutions or suggestions:

1. **Spirituality**: All spiritual paths teach the oneness of the Universe and the fraternity of humanity. In many cases, religious doctrine has been used to subjugate peoples, especially the indigenous peoples of the Americas and Africans. Use your spirituality as a tool and

guide to be aware of your behavior and make changes when necessary.

2. **Courage**: Being a potential white ally requires courage. It requires courage to confront a system from which you have been (and continue to be) a direct or indirect beneficiary. When you realize how white imperialism has adversely impacted the planet, you have a choice. You can either go along to get along. Or, you can stand up and denounce the injustices being placed on melanoid people. Understand that when you take a stand, you put your white privilege (and white life) on the line. Everything in Nature has a price tag. What are you willing to pay? I recommend all potential white allies to watch the movie **CRY FREEDOM** starring Kevin Kline and Denzel Washington. This movie is about the

relationship between white journalist Donald Woods and South African activist Bantu Steven Biko. This movie depicts the risks Woods took to get Biko's story to the world and the adversities he faced as a white ally of the anti-apartheid movement.

3. **Study Melanoid Peoples**: How many melanoid memoirs have you read? Have you read Assata Shakur's **ASSATA**? Huey P. Newton's **REVOLUTIONARY SUICIDE**? Kwame Nkrumah's **HANDBOOK OF REVOLUTIONARY WARFARE**? An effective ally must hear the lion's side of history. Too often, the hunter was the narrator. Now, the lion has his day in court. When you hear the lion's story from the lion itself, it allows you to have a more balanced view of the world and world events.

4. **Take Action**: Figure out what role you can play as an ally. More importantly, be a **proactive** ally. Host a viewing of the **EYES ON THE PRIZE** series at a local community center or local library. Attend local political meetings to learn how certain public policies impact melanoid people in your area.

5. **Volunteer**: Find an event or series of events where you can volunteer. It can be cultural, political, or another form of event. Be aware of your feelings as you dwell amongst people of other hues, religions, and languages. Do you feel "out of place"? If so, why? Your self-awareness and self-discovery will help in your development as an ally…and a human being.

6. **Be Pro-Human**: Potential white allies must be driven by a "pro-human" agenda instead of

an "anti-racism" agenda. In Godfather III, Michael Corleone warns his nephew, Vincent, to "never hate your enemy. It affects your judgment." Che Guevara teaches that the true revolutionary is motivated and driven by love. Your love of humanity must be stronger than your anger, rage, bitterness, and resentment towards racism and white hegemony. Love will cast out fear in a critical moment.

7. **The Healing Process cannot be driven by Whites**: There seems to be a tendency (consciously or unconsciously) for whites to attempt to define and dictate how those victimized by racism and white imperialism should respond and the path they should take to heal. For the past 500 years, whites have abused and misused the power bestowed upon them. Therefore, you are in **NO** moral

position to advise those affected by white imperialism on how healing should take place. It will be viewed as another means of white domination. Too much blood is on your hands. What you can do is assist those who are participating in the grieving and healing of the trauma of the Maafa ("great disaster" in Swahili).

8. **Whites cannot pick our friends or leaders**: An ally cannot dictate who is a friend or foe to melanoid peoples. For example, Fidel Castro has been a friend to African people since he came to power in Cuba in 1959. He has assisted freedom fighters in Angola against the Portuguese, as well as the Algerian revolution against the French. Castro was very instrumental in the dismantling of apartheid in South Africa.

Venezuelan President Hugo Chavez has given poor people in the Bronx free oil and kerosene. Who you may call an "enemy" maybe our friend.

9. **Process before the Prize**: Healing is a process, not a special moment. The healing journey has no shortcuts or skipping steps. Everyone wants peace and love. Yet those who want to assist in the healing journey underestimate the severity of the damage done and refuse to invest the necessary work healing requires. There must be a space of emotional safety for expressions of grief, anger, rage, sadness, and the release of pain. Those traumatized by colonialism and terrorism must go through the process of healing. There are times when that healing will get ugly and messy. There

are times when people will feel fatigued from the detoxification of such intense emotions.

10. **Appropriate Forgiveness**: When Dylan Roof killed nine African people in a church in Charleston, SC, many people, and the press demanded that Roof be forgiven for his transgressions. The problem is that premature and inappropriate forgiveness prevents true healing. Why are African people made to be unreasonably moral in their suffering? When you use premature and immature forgiveness as a means to sweep the issue under the rug, you set the climate for an explosive situation that will be uncompromising and without mercy.

11. **Be willing to "snitch"**: An elder once taught me that a good white ally must be willing to tell a melanoid person what is said about

melanoid people in private. I think a more accurate term is "debrief". More importantly, does a potential white ally challenge and counter negative comments and behaviors by whites in our absence?

12. **Study other "Allies":** John Brown, Wendy Day, Jane Elliot, John Potash, Gary Webb, and Donald Woods are the prototypes of what is a white ally. Each has paid a tremendous price for standing up for the rights of African people. Yet, they stood strong in their convictions. A potential white ally must never underestimate the price to pay and the extent to how far white hegemony will go to crush any and all opposition.

13. **Find your Niche**: Dr. Neely Fuller and the late Dr. Frances Cress Welsing discuss how there are nine areas of people activity that have

been infected with racism/white hegemony: 1) economics, 2) education, 3) entertainment (propaganda), 4) labor, 5) law, 6) politics, 7) religion, 8) sex, and 9) war. They also classify the human family into three categories: 1) white people, 2) non-white people, and 3) racists and white supremacists. As a white ally, you can study each area of human activity and see where your skill sets intersect with the specific area. I would also add a tenth area of people activity: health and medicine.

14. **Focus on your "why" before the "how-to"**: Sometimes, the white ally can be obsessed with the process, or "how-to" in bringing about change. Before that step, the first step is to ask yourself "why". Why am I willing to assist those victimized by racism and white hegemony? Why am I willing to place my

white privilege and white life on the line in opposition to a system from which I have been a direct or indirect beneficiary? What is my Driving Force in choosing to be an agent for Universal Justice? These questions will help you be honest about your intentions. Once you are clear about your intentions and Driving Force, you can begin the journey from "white ally" to "human rights activist".

15. **Exorcism**: Your activism as a potential white ally will lead you into the desert as the Israelites were. During this time in the desert, you will experience an exorcism. You will experience "withdrawal symptoms" from your addiction to racism, white hegemony, and the "fruits of Babylon". I can only imagine how you feel having the demonic

spirit of racism cast out of your mind, body, and soul.

16. **Reparations**: This is a topic that has been a hot button for years. The discussion of reparations has triggered a variety of emotions from various sides. European Jews have received reparations for the human suffering they experienced in Nazi Germany and persecution in the old USSR. Native Americans receive reparations via casinos and other benefits. Yet, African people are fighting for Congress to have a conversation about it. As part of the healing process, African people need resources to do for themselves and become whole and self-sufficient. America got 310 years of free labor out of enslaved Africans. The 40 Acres, two mules, and $100 promised by the Freedmen's Bureau were denied when Andrew Johnson took office after Abraham

> Lincoln's assassination and dismantled the bureau. The potential white ally must know that reparations are more than money. It's about settling a debt owed to a people who gave free labor to build the "Pax Americana" empire.

As a potential ally, always remember your position. When you are a guest in someone else's house, act like one. In fact, I recommend that you bring a small gift as a sign of gratitude. There is more I can possibly say, but this should be sufficient for now.

Sincerely,

Brother Minister Zumbi Y. Shawala, S.O.A.P.

(Servant of African People)

Call To Action

CALL TO ACTION

Now that you've read the first installment of the G.O.A.T. series, you have all 60 principles, Core Beliefs, and Commandments at your disposal. Creating the G.O.A.T. philosophy was no small feat. I've invested over twenty years in educating myself about business, economics, finance, and entrepreneurship. Twelve of those years were invested in building and revising this philosophy and system. I even used myself as a guinea pig and applied various G.O.A.T. principles to transform my financial life.

So, what is your next step? What do you do now? Once you've read the book, you must put the book into action. As the reader, you must become a scientist and pressure test the principles of G.O.A.T. Many people will read it and place it on the shelf, not even putting one principle to the test. I need feedback to know if people are having success. I also need to know if there is room to improve and sharpen the G.O.A.T. system and philosophy.

Some steps that can be immediately taken include:

1. **Begin practicing the 10% Solution**: A portion of all you make is yours to keep. Begin to learn to live on 90% of your income. As you increase your income, you can store more money and live on less.
2. **Set a goal to save or raise $1000 over a 90-day or 12-week period**: This is the first challenge that a wealth builder should embrace. The main point is not so much the amount saved, but who you must become to put it into practice.
3. **Create a "side hustle" to raise capital for future endeavors**: The side hustle is primarily

> to raise capital to finance future projects. Regardless of the industry, the wealth builder must always remember that he is in the moneymaking business.

I humbly come before African people with a system to help lift us out of poverty and place us in a prosperous position and condition. The future of African people is hanging in the balance. I urge you to put this book to the test. It works only if you work with it.

The biggest thing is finding a purpose and Driving Force of putting the G.O.A.T. to work. When you discover that purpose and Driving Force, you will transform your financial life and see a drastic improvement. If you find out a strong enough "why", you will discover any "how." All revolutions and personal transformations begin with the man in the mirror. Be the change you desire to experience in your business and personal financial life.

Thank you for reading and supporting this black economic liberation theology.

Suggested Reading List

SUGGESTED READING LIST

"Wealth is the result of man's capacity to think."

Ayn Rand

I've always believed whenever I give a presentation, I should always give two things to the audience: 1) Material for further study and 2) Reading List or Bibliography. When I began developing a suggested reading list for this chapter, I had to think about books that I feel will help the reader in his wealth-building journey. The list is a combination of African and non-African authors. The African authors are primarily for framing an African-centered paradigm towards business, economics, and finance. The non-African authors provide the technical skill sets necessary to achieve financial freedom and economic independence.

The Qur'an teaches man to "study the Universe, for those who seek knowledge seek the pleasure of Allah

(God)". As aspiring wealth builders, African people should always seek an advantage in building their financial empires. Even the Honorable Marcus Garvey encouraged his followers to engage in four hours of productive reading daily to become an expert in one's field. Hopefully, this reading list will improve your expertise in creating, building, protecting, and bequeathing your wealth. Happy Reading! ☺

- **BUSINESS PLAN IN A DAY** by Rhonda Abrams
- **ENTREPRENEURSHIP: A REAL-WORLD APPROACH** by Rhonda Abrams
- **FINDING AN ANGEL INVESTOR** by Rhonda Abrams
- **THE SUCCESSFUL BUSINESS PLAN** by Rhonda Abrams
- **SIX-WEEK STARTUP** by Rhonda Abrams

- **EIGHT PILLARS OF PROSPERITY** by James Allen
- **MULTIPLE STREAMS OF INCOME** by Robert Allen
- **ZERO TO ONE MILLION** by Ryan P. Allis
- **BLACK LABOR WHITE WEALTH** by Claud Anderson, Ed.D
- **POWERNOMICS** by Claud Anderson, Ed.D
- **AFRICA RISING** by Keidi Obi Awadu
- **FUTURENOMICS** by Keidi Obi Awadu
- **THE BLACKEST SOIL** by Keidi Obi Awadu
- **MOVING BEYOND RACE-ISM** by Keidi Obi Awadu
- **THE NEW SCRAMBLE FOR AFRICA** by Keidi Obi Awadu
- **THE REPAIRING** by Keidi Obi Awadu
- **THE ROAD TO POWER** by Keidi Obi Awadu
- **THE MYTH AND PROPAGANDA OF BLACK BUYING POWER** by Jared A. Ball, PhD

- **BIG BUCKS!** By Ken Blanchard and Sheldon Bowles
- **LIVE YOUR DREAMS** by Les Brown
- **THE SUCCESS PRINCIPLES** by Jack Canfield
- **THE POWER OF FOCUS** by Jack Canfield, Mark Victor Hansen, and Les Hewitt
- **THE 10X RULE** by Grant Cardone
- **SELL OR BE SOLD** by Grant Cardone
- **THE MILLIONAIRE BOOKLET** by Grant Cardone
- **IF YOU'RE NOT FIRST YOU'RE LAST** by Grant Cardone
- **HOW TO WIN FRIENDS AND INFLUENCE PEOPLE** by Dale Carnegie
- **NOTES FOR AN AFRICAN WORLD REVOLUTION** by Dr. John Henrik Clarke
- **THE RICHEST MAN IN BABYLON** by George S. Clason
- **BLACKONOMICS** by James Clingman, Jr., PhD

- **WEALTH 101** by Wade B. Cook
- **RICH HABITS** by Tom Corely
- **THE 7 HABITS OF HIGHLY EFFECTIVE PEOPLE** by Steven Covey
- **THE BARON SON** by Vicky T. Davis, William R. Patterson, and D. Marques Patton
- **REVEALING THE SECRETS OF THE GAME** by W. James Dennis
- **UNLOCKING THE SMALL BUSINESS GAME** by W. James Dennis
- **THE WISDOM OF FINANCE** by Mihir Desali
- **SECRETS OF THE MILLIONAIRE MIND** by T. Harv Eker
- **THE 4-HOUR WORKWEEK** by Tim Ferris
- **TOOL OF TITANS** by Tim Ferris
- **TRIBE OF MENTORS** by Tim Ferris
- **THE BLACK FINANCIAL LITERACY & WEALTH BUILDING BIBLE** by David Fontaine

- **RISE OF THE ROBOTS** by Martin Ford
- **CLICK** by George C. Fraser
- **SUCCESS RUNS IN OUR RACE** by George C. Fraser
- **WHY YOU'RE BROKE, DUMB AND STUPID** by Randy Gage
- **AWAKEN THE ENTREPRENEUR WITHIN** by Michael Gerber
- **E-MYTH MASTERY** by Michael Gerber
- **THE E-MYTH ENTERPRISE** by Michael Gerber
- **THE E-MYTH REVISITED** by Michael Gerber
- **THE MOST SUCCESSFUL SMALL BUSINESS IN THE WORLD** by Michael Gerber
- **HOW TO BE RICH** by J. Paul Getty
- **WEALTH WITHOUT RISK** by Charles J. Givens
- **MORE WEALTH WITHOUT RISK** by Charles J. Givens
- **TRIBES** by Seth Godin

- **TURN YOUR PASSION INTO PROFIT** by Walt F.J. Goodridge
- **HOW TO SUCCEED IN BUSINESS WITHOUT BEING WHITE** by Earl G. Graves
- **THE 50th LAW** by Robert Greene and 50 Cent
- **KILLING SACRED COWS** by Garrett Gunderson
- **WHAT WOULD THE ROCKEFELLERS DO** by Garrett Gunderson
- **THE ENTREPRENEURIAL ROLLER COASTER** by Darren Hardy
- **THE 12 UNIVERSAL LAWS OF SUCCESS** by Herbert Harris
- **THE LAWS OF SUCCESS** by Napoleon Hill
- **THINK & GROW RICH** by Napoleon Hill
- **THE POWER OF BROKE** by Daymond John
- **RISE & GRIND** by Daymond John
- **TURN SETBACKS INTO GREENBACKS** by Dr. Willie Jolley

- **THINK & GROW RICH: A BLACK CHOICE** by Dennis Kimbro, PhD
- **THE WEALTH CHOICE** by Dennis Kimbro, PhD
- **WHAT MAKES THE GREAT GREAT** By Dennis Kimbro, PhD
- **THE ART OF THE START 2.0** by Guy Kawasaki
- **LOOPHOLES OF THE RICH** by Diane Kennedy, CPA
- **RICH WOMAN** by Kim Kiyosaki
- **RICH DAD POOR DAD** by Robert T. Kiyosaki
- **CASHFLOW QUADRANT** by Robert T. Kiyosaki
- **RICH DAD'S GUIDE TO INVESTING** by Robert T. Kiyosaki
- **RICH DAD'S INCREASE YOUR FINANCIAL IQ** by Robert T. Kiyosaki
- **BEFORE YOU QUIT YOUR JOB** by Robert T. Kiyosaki

- **FAKE** by Robert T. Kiyosaki
- **THE RAVENS** by Robert T. Kiyosaki and James Rickards
- **WHO STOLE MY PENSION** by Robert T. Kiyosaki and Edward Siedle
- **MAKE YOUR KID A MONEY GENIUS** by Beth Kobliner
- **TRIBES** by Joel A. Kotkin
- **GRINDING IT OUT: THE MAKING OF McDONALD'S** by Ray Kroc
- **THE MILLIONAIRE MAKER** by Loral Langemeier
- **THE MILLIONAIRE MAKER'S GUIDE TO CREATING A CASH MACHINE FOR LIFE** by Loral Langemeier
- **THE MILLIONAIRE MAKER'S GUIDE TO WEALTH CYCLE INVESTING** by Loral Langemeier

- **BUSINESS SECRETS FROM THE BIBLE** by Rabbi Daniel Lapin
- **THOU SHALL PROSPER** by Rabbi Daniel Lapin
- **MONEY IS MY FRIEND** by Phil Laut with Lisa Kitter and Jeffery Combs
- **GUERRILLA MARKETING** by Jay Conrad Levinson
- **WHY SHOULD WHITE GUYS HAVE ALL THE FUN** by Reginald Lewis
- **THE 10% ENTREPRENEUR** by Patrick McGinnis
- **HOW TO TURN $100 INTO $1,000,000** by James McKenna and Jeannine Glista
- **PSYCHO-CYBERNETICS** by Maxwell Maltz, MD
- **AUTOMATIC WEALTH** by Michael Masterson
- **READY, FIRE, AIM** by Michael Masterson

- **SEVEN YEARS TO SEVEN FIGURES** by Michael Masterson
- **DIGITALNOMICS** by Philippe SHOCK Matthews
- **GUARANTEED SUCCESS** by Percy "Master P" Miller
- **THE ENTREPRENEURIAL SECRET (Vol. 1-3)** by Cedric Muhammad
- **AN ECONOMIC BLUEPRINT FOR BLACK AMERICA** by The Most Honorable Elijah Muhammad
- **COMMONOMICS: DEVELOPING A POST YAKUB ECONOMY** by Dr. Ridgely A. Mu'Min Muhammad
- **COMMONOMICS II: THE SHEEP, SHEEPDOG AND THE EVIL SHEPHERD** by Dr. Ridgely A. Mu'Min Muhammad
- **THE POWER OF YOUR SUBCONSCIOUS MIND** by Joseph Murphy, PhD

- **THE BOOK OF FIVE RINGS** by Miyamoto Musashi
- **BECOMING YOUR OWN BANKER: UNLOCK THE INFINITE BANKING CONCEPT** by R. Nelson Nash
- **BUILDING YOUR WAREHOUSE OF WEALTH** by R. Nelson Nash
- **THE ROBOTS ARE COMING!** By Andres' Oppenheimer
- **THE POWER OF POSITIVE THINKING** by Norman Vincent Peale
- **OBJECTIVISM: THE PHILOSOPHY OF AYN RAND** by leonard Peikoff
- **CAMPUS CEO** by Randall Pinkett, Ph.D
- **BLACK FACES IN WHITE PLACES** by Randall Pinkett and John Robinson
- **THE ART AND SCIENCE OF RESPECT** by J Prince

- **THE ROBOTS ARE COMING** by John Pugliano
- **ATLAS SHRUGGED** by Ayn Rand
- **CAPITALISM: THE UNKNOWN IDEAL** by Ayn Rand
- **THE VIRTUE OF SELFISHNESS** by Ayn Rand
- **AFTERMATH** by James Rickards
- **CURRENCY WARS** by James Rickards
- **THE DEATH OF MONEY** by James Rickards
- **THE NEW CASE FOR GOLD** by James Rickards
- **THE NEW GREAT DEPRESSION** by James Rickards
- **THE ROAD TO RUIN** by James Rickards
- **THE ONE-PAGE PROPOSAL** by Patrick G. Riley
- **THE END OF WORK** by Jeremy Rifkin
- **UNLIMITED POWER** by Anthony Robbins
- **THE BLACK TAX** by Shawn Rochester

- **CREATING MONEY: ATTRACTING ABUNDANCE** by Sanaya Roman & Duane Packer
- **MILLION DOLLAR HABITS** by Robert J. Ringer
- **RIDIN' WITH RICK: THE 21 KEYS OF SUCCESS** by "Freeway" Rick Ross and Kolie Crutcher
- **STARTUP NATION** by Jeff & Richard Sloan
- **MONEY ISSUES IN BLACK MALE/FEMALE RELATIONSHIPS** by George Subira
- **GOALS** by Brian Tracy
- **THE ART OF LEADERSHIP (Vol. 1-2)** by Oba T'Shaka
- **REVOLUTIONARY WEALTH** by Alvin & Heidi Toffler
- **EVANGELPRENEUR** by Josh Tolley
- **QUIT YOUR JOB OR DIE** by Josh Tolley
- **THE ART OF WAR** by Sun Tzu

- **THE PSYCHOLOGY OF WINNING** by Dennis Waitley, PhD
- **CHARACTER BUILDING** by Booker T. Washington
- **BLUEPRINT FOR BLACK POWER** by Amos Wilson, PhD
- **THE WAR ON NORMAL PEOPLE** by Andrew Yang
- **BANKER TO THE POOR** by Muhammad Yunus, PhD
- **CREATING A WORLD WITHOUT POVERTY** by Muhammad Yunus, PhD
- **BUILDING SOCIAL BUSINESS** by Muhammad Yunus, PhD
- **A WORLD OF THREE ZEROS** by Muhammad Yunus, PhD
- **MORE MONEY NOW** by Michael Zechmann

GLOSSARY

40% Rule: According to Grant Cardone, an individual must earn enough money to save (40%) as much as he pays in taxes (40% in state and federal); work to store 40% of gross revenue/income for a future investment

- **Accounting**: Process of recording financial transactions of a business
- **Accounting Equation**: Assets = Liabilities + Shareholders' Equity
- **Acquisition**: One company purchases all or most of the other company's shares to gain control of that company
- **Active Income**: Income received from performing a service; includes wages, tips, salaries, and commissions

- **Angel Investor**: Individual who provides capital for a startup business in exchange for convertible debt or ownership equity; usually offers technical assistance at the initial phases of the startup business
- **Annual Percentage Rate (APR)**: Annual rate of interest charged to borrowers and paid to investors; associated with mortgages, loans, and credit cards
- **Appreciation**: The increased value of an asset over time
- **Asset**: Resource with economic value that an individual, corporation that a nation owns or controls with the expectation of providing a future benefit
- **Balance Sheet**: One of three major financial statements that include assets, liabilities, the equity capital of a business or other organization

- **Bank**: Financial institution that accepts deposits from the public and creates a demand deposit, while simultaneously making loans
- **Bankruptcy**: Legal proceeding involving a person or business that is unable to repay its outstanding debts
- **Barter**: Act of trading goods between two parties without the use of money
- **Bear Market**: Condition of a financial market in which the market experiences declined prices over a prolonged period; usually influenced by negative investor sentiment and declining economic prospects
- **"Black Hand" Theory**: The people who are rarely seen, heard, or discussed are the true shot callers, policymakers, and check writers (e.g. David Rockefeller)
- **Boiler Room**: Place of operation (call center) where high-pressure salespeople call lists of

potential investors ("sucker lists")to peddle speculative and/or fraudulent securities

- **Bond**: A loan to a company or government that pays investors a fixed rate of return over a specific period
- **Bootstrapping**: Launching a business with little or no outside cash investment or other support
- **Bottom Line**: Refers to a company's earnings, profits, net income, or earnings per share
- **Brand**: Identifying symbol, mark, logo, name, word, and/or sentence that companies use to distinguish their products from others
- **Brand Awareness**: Familiarity of consumers with a particular product or service
- **Brand Loyalty**: Demonstrated by repeat purchases of a product even when the consumer has choices of competing alternatives

- **Brand Recognition**: Ability of consumers to identify a specific brand by its attributes over another brand
- **Budget**: Plan or estimate of the amount of money needed for a specific purpose; estimation of revenue and expenses over a specified future period
- **Budget Deficit**: When expenses exceed revenue and indicate the financial health of a nation
- **Budget Surplus**: Period when income exceeds expenditures; displays the financial health of a nation (indicates the effective management of a government)
- **Bull Market**: Condition of a financial market in which prices rise or expect to rise; the term used primarily in the stock market
- **Business**: An organization involved in the trade of goods, services, or both, to customers and clients

- **Business Exit Strategy**: An entrepreneur's strategic plan to sell his or her ownership in a company to investors of another company
- **Business Model**: A company's strategy to turn a profit; includes how a business makes money, how it operates, and who its target market is
- **Business Plan**: A written document that describes how a business (specifically a startup) defines its objectives and lays out its strategy to achieve its goals and objectives
- **Business to Business (B2B)**: Transaction between businesses (e.g. manufacturer and wholesale distributor)
- **Business to Consumer (B2C)**: Process of selling products and services directly between a business and its consumers who are the end-users

- **Business to Government (B2G)**: Sales and marketing of products and services to federal, state, county, and local agencies
- **Capital**: Wealth in the form of money or other assets by an individual, business, or other organization; assets that can enhance one's power to perform economically useful work
- **Capital Gains**: Profit from the sale of property or other investment
- **Capitalism**: Economic system in which private individuals or businesses own capital goods
- **Cash on Delivery (C.O.D.)**: Transaction in which the recipient makes a payment for a good at the time of delivery
- **Cash Reserve**: The money a company or individual keeps on hand to address any short-term and emergency needs
- **Cashflow Management**: Process of tracking how much money comes into and goes out of

one's business; helps predict how much money will be available to one's business in the future

- **Cashflow Statement:** One of three major financial statements that provide aggregate data of all cash inflows that a company receives from its ongoing operations and external investment sources; include all cash outflows that pay for business activities and investments during a specific period
- **Code of Ethics:** Guide of principles designed to help professionals conduct business honestly and with integrity
- **Collateral**: Asset that a lender accepts as security for a loan
- **Commodity**: A basic good used in commerce that is interchangeable with other goods of the same type (e.g. gold, silver, etc.)

- **Compound Interest**: Interest that accrues on the initial principal and the accumulated interest of a principal deposit, loan, or debt
- **Corporation**: Company or group of people authorized to act as a single entity and recognized as such in law
- **Cost**: Monetary value of goods and services
- **Cost of Goods Sold (COGS)**: Direct costs of producing goods sold by a company
- **Creative Destruction**: Dismantling of long-standing practices in order to make way for innovation; coined by Austrian economist Joseph Schumpter in 1942
- **Credit**: Ability of a customer to obtain goods and services before payment
- **Credit Union**: Non-Profit money cooperative whose members can borrow from pooled deposits at low-interest rates

- **Cryptocurrency**: Digital asset designed to work as a medium of exchange and secured by cryptography, which is virtually impossible to counterfeit or double-spend
- **Culture**: Characteristics and knowledge of a particular group of people encompassing language, religion, cuisine, social habits, music, and arts; shared patterns of behaviors and interactions, cognitive constructs, and understanding that are learned by socialization
- **Debt**: Obligation that requires one party (the debtor) to pay money or other mutually agreed value to another party (the creditor); deferred payment that differentiates immediate payment
- **Depreciation**: Reduction in the value of an asset over time, primarily through wear and tear

- **Depression**: An extreme recession that lasts three or more years or which leads to a decline in the real gross domestic product (GDP)
- **Direct Deposit**: Deposit of funds electronically into a bank account rather than through a physical paper check
- **Dividend**: Distribution of profits by a corporation to its shareholders; issued as cash, stocks, or another form of asset
- **Earned Income**: Money derived from paid work, either as an employee or as a self-employed individual
- **Economics**: Science that addresses the production, distribution, and consumption of goods and services, or the material welfare of humanity

- **Economy**: The way a community, country, nation, or empire manages its money and other resources (e.g., labor, land, equipment) to produce, buy and sell goods and services
- **Economic Development**: Creation of wealth from which community benefits are realized; an increase in a nation's wealth and standard of living; measured by the increase in the gross domestic product (GDP), which measures a nation's productivity
- **Economic Empowerment**: Ability to make and act on decisions that involve the control over and allocation of financial resources: how people work together to create wealth; development of the ability of the historically disadvantaged to engage in economic activity that benefits both the individuals in question and the broader society

- **Economic Synergy**: Concept where businesses within an economy complement each other and stimulate economic growth; also known as vertical integration

- **Entrepreneurship**: Capacity and willingness to develop, organize and manage a business venture, along with any risks, in order to make a profit

- **Entrepreneur**: Person who organizes, operates, and assumes the risk and reward for a business venture

- **Equity**: Value of shares given by a company; calculated as a company's total assets minus its total liabilities

- **ESOP**: Employee Stock Ownership Plan; employee benefit plan that gives employees and executives ownership interest (equity) in the company; usually offered through shares

- **ETF (Exchange Traded Funds)**: equity mutual fund that is listed and traded in the stock market

- **Expense**: Cost of operations a company incurs to generate revenue

- **FDIC**: Federal Deposit Insurance Corporation; one of two agencies that provide deposit insurance to depositors in U.S. depository institutions (banks)

- **Federal Reserve**: Central banking system of the United States; regulates the monetary and financial system; composed of a central government agency based in Washington, DC, Board of Governors and 12 regional Federal Reserve banks in major US cities

- **FICO Score**: An individual's credit score calculated with software from Fair, Isaacs, and Company; the score is based on the amount owed, length of credit history, and payment history
- **Fiat Money**: Government-issued currency not backed by gold or other precious metal that is accepted as a means of exchange
- **Financial IQ**: Also known as financial quotient (FQ); Ability to obtain and manage one's wealth by understanding how money works; ability to solve problems with the proper financial vehicles and tools
- **Financial Intelligence**: Ability to acquire and apply knowledge and skills gained from understanding financial and accounting principles in the business world

- **Financial Literacy**: Ability to use knowledge and skills to manage financial resources effectively for a lifetime of financial freedom and economic independence
- **Financial Statement(s)**: Written records that convey the business activities and financial performance of a company; audited by government agencies, accountants, firms, etc to ensure accuracy and for tax, financing, or investing purposes
- **Fiscal Year**: A year as reckoned for taxing or accounting purposes
- **Generational Wealth**: Assets (tangible and intangible)bequeathed from one generation to the next; tangible assets include real estate, paper assets (stocks, bonds, mutual funds, etc.), businesses, or anything else that carries monetary value; intangible assets include

money habits, lessons, and wisdom regarding business, economics, and finance

- **Gresham's Law**: Bad money drives out good
- **Gross Domestic Product (GDP)**: Also known as Gross National Product; total value of goods produced and services provided in a nation during one year
- **Gross Income**: An individual's total pay from his or her employer before taxes or other deductions
- **Gross Profit**: Gross Profit = Revenue - Cost of Goods Sold (COGS)
- **Guerrilla Marketing**: Innovative, unconventional, and low-cost marketing techniques aimed at obtaining maximum exposure of a product or service; created by Jay Conrad Levinson

- **Hard Asset**: Tangible asset or resource with a fundamental value
- **History**: Branch of knowledge dealing with past events; a continuous, systematic narrative of past events as relating to a particular people, nation, period, and person usually written as a chronological account
- **Human Capital**: Intangible asset or quality not listed on a company's balance sheet; the economic value of a worker
- **Hyperinflation**: Term used to describe rapid, excessive, and out-of-control general price increases in an economy
- **Income**: Money that an individual or business receives in exchange for providing goods and services through investing capital

- **Income Statement**: AKA Profit & Loss Statement; one of three major financial statements that display a company's revenues and expenses over a specific period; Net Income= (Total Revenue + Gains) – (Total Expenses + Losses)
- **Infinite Banking Concept**: Created by Nelson Nash; the process by which an individual becomes his banker by funding whole life insurance policies and "borrowing from yourself"
- **Inflation**: General increase in prices and fall in the purchasing power of money
- **Informal Economy**: Economic activity that is neither taxed nor monitored by a government or other municipality

- **Intaxification**: Feeling of satisfaction and joy that one feels upon receiving his or her tax refund; feeling is arguably misguided because the refund is the result of the individual paying too much taxes in the previous year
- **Interest**: Charge for the privilege of borrowing money, typically expressed as annual percentage rate (APR)
- **IRA (Individual Retirement Account)**: Tax-advantaged investment tool for individuals to earmark their retirement savings; usually invested with pre-tax money
- **Kaizen**: Japanese term meaning "change for the better" or "continuous improvement"; Japanese business philosophy regarding the processes that continuously improve operations and involve all employees

- **Kickback**: Illegal payment intended as compensation for preferential treatment or any other type of improper services received
- **Knowledge Capital**: Value of an organization made up of its knowledge, relationships, learned techniques, procedures, and innovations
- **Liability**: Something owed by an individual or a company; financial obligations of a company owed to creditors
- **Limited Liability Company**: Business structure in the US whereby the owners are not personally liable for its debts or liabilities; a hybrid entity that combines the characteristics of a corporation with those of a partnership or sole proprietorship

- **Liquidity**: Ease of converting an asset or security into cash
- **Loan**: Money that is given to the other party (usually by a financial institution) in exchange for the repayment of the principal plus interest
- **Marketing**: Action or business of promoting products and services, including market research and advertising
- **Market Price**: Current Price at which goods and services can be purchased or sold
- **Market Share**: Percent of total sales in an industry generated by a particular company
- **Means of Production**: Physical non-human inputs used in production (assets used to produce wealth; e.g., machinery, tools,

factories); raw materials and means of labor employed in the production process

- **Merger**: Agreement that unites two existing companies into one new company
- **Microfinance**: Banking Service provided to unemployed and low-income individuals or groups who otherwise would have no other access to financial services
- **Microloan**: Small sum of money lent at a low-interest rate to a new business
- **Money**: Current medium of exchange in the form of coins and banknotes; also called currency or cash
- **Money Freedom**: Having the financial resources to cover one's financial expenses and obligations throughout one's life: the ability to live on passive income sources

gained through active income efforts, intending to build a "walk away wealth system"

- **Money Manager**: Person or financial firm that manages the securities portfolio of an individual or institutional investor
- **Monopoly**: When a company and its products and services dominate a sector or industry
- **Mutual Fund**: Type of financial vehicle made up of a pool of money collected from many investors to invest in securities like stocks, bonds, money market instruments, and other assets that are handled by money managers
- **NCUA**: National Credit Union Association; one of two agencies that provide deposit insurance to depositors in U.S. depository institutions (credit unions)

- **Net Worth**: Sum of all assets owned by an individual or company minus any obligations or liabilities

- **Pareto Principle**: Also known as the 80/20 Rule; states that 80% of results (output) come from 20% of effort (input)

- **Partnership**: Formal arrangement by two or more parties to manage and operate a business and share its profits.

- **Passive Income**: Income that requires little to no effort to maintain; includes royalties from the usage of intellectual property, rental income, and business activities that do not require a physical presence to earn income.

- **Petty Cash**: Small amount of cash on hand used for paying expenses too small to merit writing a check.

- **Policy**: A definite or method of action selected to guide and determine present and future decisions; a principle or protocol to guide decisions and achieve rational outcomes; mostly a statement of intent and is implemented as a procedure or protocol.
- **Portfolio**: Range of investments held by an individual or organization
- **Portfolio Income**: Money received from investments, dividends, interest, and capital gains; receives more favorable tax treatment than earned income
- **Positive Imbalance**: Financial condition when an individual's financial statement reflects the assets and income/revenue is greater than expenses and liabilities

- **Power**: Ability or capacity to act or produce business activities that do not require a physical presence effect; possession of control, authority, or influence over others
- **Price**: Amount of money to be paid for a product or service; a measure of value
- **Principal**: Total amount of money borrowed or invested, excluding interest or dividends
- **Productivity**: Measures how efficiently production inputs (labor, capital) are being used in an economy to produce a given level of output
- **Profit**: Financial gain from business activity minus expenses; calculated as revenue minus expenses
- **Recession**: Significant decline in economic activity spread across the market, lasting

more than two consecutive quarters of negative gross domestic product (GDP)

- **Residual Income**: Amount of leftover operating profit after paying all costs of capital used to generate the income or revenue
- **Return on Investment (ROI)**: Ratio between net profit and the cost of investment
- **Revenue**: Income generated from normal business operations; includes discounts and deductions for returned merchandise; also known as gross sales
- **Revenue Model**: Conceptual structure that states and explains the revenue earning strategy of a business; includes sources of revenue, revenue generation techniques,

products and/or services of value, and target customer of the product/service offered.

- **ROTH IRA**: Special individual retirement account where after-tax income is invested into the investment vehicle; funds are withdrawn tax-free; created in 1997 and named after former Delaware senator William Roth
- **Sales**: Exchange of a product or service for money or other assets
- **Security**: Certificate or another financial instrument that has monetary value and can be traded
- **SEC**; Securities and Exchange Commission; independent US federal government regulatory agency responsible for protecting

investors; created in the wake of the Great Depression and 1929 Stock Market Crash

- **Seed Capital**: Type of funding used in financing a startup; usually provided by an angel investor in exchange for equity in the startup company
- **SEP IRA**: (Simplified Employee Pension Individual Retirement Account) Retirement savings plan established by business owners for the benefit of their employees and themselves; contributions are usually significantly higher than traditional IRA's
- **Shareholder**: Also known as stockholder; person, company, or institution that owns at least one share of a company's stock (equity)
- **Sole Proprietorship**: An unincorporated business owned and operated by one owner

with no distinction between the business and its owner; also known as "doing business as" (DBA)

- **Spirituality**: Sense of connection to something greater than oneself
- **Stock**: Goods or merchandise kept on the premises of a business or warehouse and available for sale or distribution; securities that represent a share in a company
- **Susu**: Means "plan" in the Akan language; a form of a rotating savings and credit association; type of informal savings club arrangement amongst a small group of people who take turns by "throwing hands"; used in the Caribbean but originates in West Africa

- **Tax**: Levy imposed by a government for the purchases of goods and services and on the income of persons and businesses
- **Tax Bracket**: A range of incomes taxed at a given rate
- **Tax Code**: A federal government document that details the rules that persons and businesses must follow in remitting a percentage of their income or revenue to the state and federal government
- **Time Freedom**: Having the freedom to move deliberately through the world without concern for the need for a paycheck
- **Trust**: Fiduciary relationship in which one party (trustor) gives another party (trustee) the right to hold property or assets for the benefit of a third party (beneficiary)

- **Unearned Income**: Income from investments and other sources unrelated to employment; income not acquired through working
- **Value**: Determination of the price of goods and services; what the customer is willing to pay for a product or service
- **Value Creation**: Performance of actions that increase the value of products, services, or businesses
- **Venture Capital**: Capital invested in a project in which there is a substantial element of risk, typically a new or expanding business
- **Vertical Integration**: Strategy used by a company to own and control the manufacturing, distribution, and retail aspects of the supply chain or the value of the product

- **Wall Street**: Eight-block long street in the financial district of Lower Manhattan; home of the New York Stock Exchange (NYSE)
- **Working Capital**: Capital of a business which is used in its daily operations; calculated as current assets minus current liabilities

About the Author

About the Author

Brother Minister Zumbi Y. Shawala (Chris Johnson, B.Msc) is the founder of Liberty Hall Media Group and the architect of the **GOSPEL OF AFRONOMICS THEOLOGY** (G.O.A.T.) philosophy and program. He is also developing a goal-setting program entitled **MVP GOALS**. Brother Minister has built a following through an online radio show called **FROM MIND 2 MARKET** from 2007-12 on LIBRadio (**www.LIBRadio.com**) with Keidi Obi Awadu.

As a business and financial thought leader, Brother Minister's philosophy is that, for people to become fiscally responsible for their lives, they must be empowered personally with the proper tools, value systems, and mindset to solve their financial problems. He also believes in "transformation" as opposed to "reformation" on a personal and professional level. So, to achieve something never achieved, a person has to become someone s/he has never been before.

In his role as an "Afronomicist" and "Afrofuturist," Brother Minister addresses the economic issues of the urban and hip-hop communities, as well as the African Diaspora from an empowerment position. He feels that these communities have the right and obligation to empower and enrich themselves to fulfill their economic destinies through microenterprise, entrepreneurship, and "community angel investing."

Brother Minister is presently a doctoral candidate for Metaphysical Studies at the University of Metaphysics in Sedona, AZ. He is a 2004 graduate of Sage College of Albany (Albany, NY) with a bachelor's degree in Interdisciplinary Studies and received a bachelor's degree in Metaphysical Science in 2012 from the University of Metaphysics, where he received his ordinance as a minister of metaphysical science.

Brother Minister presently resides in Albany, NY.

For workshops, seminars, and speaking engagements, contact Brother Minister at 518.512.9972 or **libertyhallpress@gmail.com**

About Liberty Hall Media Group

About Liberty Hall Media Group

Liberty Hall Media Group is an Albany, NY-based multimedia company that provides products and services in areas of self-help, business, personal development, and cultural consciousness. Its commitment is to the empowerment of the customer and client. Liberty Hall also offers products and services that address the unique economic, personal, and collective challenges of the African Diaspora.

Its founder, Chris Johnson (Brother Minister Zumbi Y. Shawala), saw the need to create educational products and services that can empower the client/customer to transform his personal and professional life. Mr. Johnson is the architect of G.O.A.T. (Gospel of Afronomics

Theology), which is an economic philosophy geared towards the economic empowerment of African people for the 21st century and beyond, and **MVP GOALS**, a goal-setting program that helps the individual set and achieve goals based on a clearly defined mission, vision, and purpose.

Empowerment Quotes

"History shows that it does not matter who is in power…those who have not learned to do for themselves and have to depend solely on others never obtain any more rights or privileges in the end than they did in the beginning."

Dr. Carter G. Woodson

"It is the fool whose own tomatoes are sold to him."

Akan Proverb

"God will not drive flies away from a tailless cow."

African Proverb

"People who bite the hand that feeds them usually lick the boot that kicks them."

Eric Hoffer

"POWER is the only argument that satisfies a man."

The Honorable Marcus Garvey

"Nations are built by people, but empires are built by families."

Professor Kaba Hiawatha Kamene

"If you don't control your dollar, you can never control your community."

Killer Mike

Co-Founder, Bank Greenwood

"Get rich. That is the best way you can help the poor."

Wallace D. Wattles

THE SCIENCE OF GETTING RICH

"Power never takes a back step...only in the face of more power...Power recognizes only power, and all of them who realize this have made gains."

Baba Omowale (Malcolm X)

"The rich have their assets work for them. They have gained control over their expenses and focus on acquiring or building assets. Their businesses pay most of their expenses, and they have few, if any, personal liabilities."

Robert T. Kiyosaki

"A man cannot sit down alone to plan for prosperity."

Nigerian Proverb

"If cash is king, then cashflow is God."

Brother Minister Zumbi Y. Shawala

"Permit me to issue and control the money of a nation, and I care not who makes its laws."

Meyer Amschel Rotschild

"Never pursue entrepreneurship for the greed of money. The whole reason to be an entrepreneur is the pursuit of freedom. That's why you do it."

Kevin O'Leary

SHARK TANK

"The rich organize their money; the poor and middle-class budget their money."

Brother Minister Zumbi Y. Shawala

"People with low financial literacy standards are often unable to take their ideas and create assets out of them."

Robert T. Kiyosaki

"Business is personal development in action."

Dr. Herbert Harris

"Money is God in action."

Rev. Ike

"Unity amongst the cattle makes the lion lie down hungry."

Swahili Proverb

"Without financial literacy, divorce rates soar, families rupture, and women stay with abusive men for financial security. A lack of jobs contributes to riots and illegal activity. Name any situation and it goes back to money. We need to focus on poverty eradication."

John Hope Bryant

CEO, Operation HOPE

"You need to build your businesses and hire your children. It's absolutely CRIMINAL to keep having babies and then sending them into somebody else's neighborhood to BEG for a job."

Dr. Claud Anderson

"Black Power minus Green Power means NO power!"

Rev. Ike

"You become financially free when your passive income exceeds your expenses."

T. Harv Eker

"If you want to be financially free, you need to become a different person than you are today and let go of whatever has held you back in the past."

Kim Kiyosaki

"Negroes think power is in voting. Power is not in voting; power is in money, having control of the major minerals and resources."

Dr. Amos Wilson

"In a time of drastic change, it is the learners who inherit the future. The learned usually find themselves equipped to live in a world that no longer exists."

Eric Hoffer

"If the Negro in the ghetto must eternally be fed by the hand that pushes him into the ghetto, he will never become strong enough to get out of the ghetto."

Dr. Carter G. Woodson

"How different would our education be if we went to school to learn to create jobs for ourselves?"

Dr. Amos Wilson

"The size of your money will be directly related to the size of the problem you solve."

Dr. George C. Fraser

"A well-paid slave is still a slave."

Curt Flood

"Contempt for money is another trick of the rich to keep the poor without it."
Michael Corleone
THE GODFATHER TRILOGY

"The distance between you and money is the problem."
Grant Cardone

"It takes courage to make money. It takes intelligence to keep it."
Brother Minister Zumbi Y. Shawala

"The entrepreneur always searches for change, responds to it and exploits it as an opportunity."
Peter F. Drucker

"You never change things by fighting the existing reality. To change something, build a new model that makes the existing model obsolete."

R. Buckminster Fuller

"While good business ideas are plentiful, many entrepreneurs struggle to understand payroll taxes, health care, and other thorny issues...In other words, they don't have the financial literacy to scale their businesses and attract investors."
Daymond John
FUBU founder and **SHARK TANK** investor

"Politics without economics is symbolism without substance."
The Most Honorable Elijah Muhammad

"Intelligence solves problems and produces money; money without financial intelligence is money soon gone."
Robert T. Kiyosaki

"If you want real multigenerational wealth, build your mind along with your money."

Brother Minister Zumbi Y. Shawala

"Powerful people never educate powerless people on how to take their power away from them. Education, as I have said before, has but one honorable purpose: that is to train the student to be a proper handler of power. At first. Power over himself or herself."

Dr. John Henrik Clarke

"Power can be taken, but not given. The process of the taking is empowerment in itself."

Gloria Steinem

"If you don't find a way to make money while you sleep, you will work until you die."

Warren Buffett

"People who cannot control their cash flow work for those who can."

Robert T. Kiyosaki

"The best boycott is to build your own."

Chuck D, Public Enemy, and Prophets of Rage

"Entrepreneurship is not an opportunity. It's a mentality. It's a mentality that does not accept the limitations of a salary. It says you don't determine how much I make. You can determine how much you're going to pay me, but you can't determine how much I'm going to make. Because how much I'm going to make is only determined by the tenacity of my own creativity."

Bishop T.D. Jakes

"In order to truly serve God, you must be financially free and economically independent of man. Being financially free and economically independent reduces the chances of having your integrity, morals, and ethics compromised."

Brother Minister Zumbi Y. Shawala

"If you give a hungry man food, he will eat it. But, if you give him land, he will grow his own food."

Fannie Lou Hamer

"Those who master money are free to serve others still mastered by it."

Orrin Woodward, Author

"Masters of money do not need money. Masters of money are alchemists. They turn ideas into gold. They turn ideas into international businesses."

Robert T. Kiyosaki

WHY THE RICH GET RICHER

(PG. 189)

"You cannot claim equality with the person who provides for your daily meals."

Akan Proverb

Powerlessness breeds a race of beggars."

Kwame Ture & Charles V. Hamilton

"You can't sustain the mission if you don't make the money."

Brendon Bruchard

EXPERTS Academy

"Why should fools have money in hand to buy wisdom, when they are not able to understand it?"

Proverbs 17:16

(Good News Translation-Holy Bible)

"Surely, Allah will not change the condition of a people until the people change it themselves."

Surah 13:11 (Holy Quran)

"Let us put our money together; let us use our money; let us put our money out at usury among ourselves, and reap the benefits among ourselves. Let us have a bank that will take the nickels and turn them into dollars."

Maggie L. Walker

"Knowledge makes a man unfit to be a slave."

Frederick Douglass

"We must understand that to be black and beautiful means nothing in this world unless we are black and powerful."

Dr. John Henrik Clarke

"Any action, regardless of its motives, is sterile unless it produces practical and concrete results."

Amilcar Cabral

He who is ruled by his appetite belongs to the enemy."

Ptahhotep

"You don't get liberated through morality. You get liberated through power."

Kwame Ture'

"We can't treat the matter of black economic empowerment as just the redistribution of existing wealth. It really has to focus on new investment, on growth, on development of employment, and so on and so on."

Former South African President Thabo Mbeki

"Equality begins with economic empowerment."

George H.W. Bush

"A poor revolutionary leads a poor revolution."

Professor Kaba Hiawatha Kamene

"Revolution is a process in progress."

Brother Minister Zumbi Y. Shawala

"As a people, we must become producers and not remain consumers and employees. We must be able to extract raw materials from the earth and manufacture them into something useful for ourselves. This would create jobs in production. We must remember that without land, there is no production. The surplus of what we produce, we would sell. This would develop a field of commerce and trade as other free and independent people whose population is less than that of the 20 million so-called Negroes who are dependent in America."

The Honorable Elijah Muhammad

MESSAGE TO THE BLACKMAN

"Leaders have devoted their time to politics, little knowing, it seems that political independence disappears without economic independence. That economic independence is the foundation of political independence."

Booker T. Washington

"Economics is the new black power."

Dr. George C. Fraser

"If you don't have a system, you don't have a business."

Dr. George C. Fraser

"The revolution will not be televised; it will be monetized."

Dr. George C. Fraser

"Poor people spend their money and invest what's left. Rich people save their money and spend what's left."

Jim Rohn

"All human beings are entrepreneurs. When we were in the caves, we were all self-employed...finding our food, feeding ourselves. That's where human history began. As civilization came, we suppressed it. We became "labor" because they stamped us. 'You are labor'. We forgot that we are entrepreneurs."

Dr. Muhammad Yunus
Founder of the Grameen Bank
and Microfinance Movement

Made in the USA
Middletown, DE
16 February 2021

33866283R00293